CAMBRIDGE PRIMARY
English

Learner's Book

Sally Burt and Debbie Ridgard

CAMBRIDGE
UNIVERSITY PRESS

University Printing House, Cambridge CB2 8BS, United Kingdom

One Liberty Plaza, 20th Floor, New York, NY 10006, USA

477 Williamstown Road, Port Melbourne, VIC 3207, Australia

314–321, 3rd Floor, Plot 3, Splendor Forum, Jasola District Centre,
New Delhi - 110025, India

79 Anson Road, #06–04/06, Singapore 079906

Cambridge University Press is part of the University of Cambridge.

It furthers the University's mission by disseminating knowledge in the pursuit of education, learning and research at the highest international levels of excellence.

Information on this title: education.cambridge.org

© Cambridge University Press 2015

This publication is in copyright. Subject to statutory exception
and to the provisions of relevant collective licensing agreements,
no reproduction of any part may take place without the written
permission of Cambridge University Press.

First published 2015

20 19 18 17 16 15 14

Printed in India by Repro India Ltd

A catalogue record for this publication is available from the British Library

ISBN 978-1-107-62866-3 Paperback

Cambridge University Press has no responsibility for the persistence or accuracy of URLs for external or third-party internet websites referred to in this publication, and does not guarantee that any content on such websites is, or will remain, accurate or appropriate. Information regarding prices, travel timetables, and other factual information given in this work is correct at the time of first printing but the publishers do not guarantee the accuracy of such information thereafter.

....

NOTICE TO TEACHERS
It is illegal to reproduce any part of this work in material form (including photocopying and electronic storage) except under the following circumstances:
(i) where you are abiding by a licence granted to your school or institution by the Copyright Licensing Agency;
(ii) where no such licence exists, or where you wish to exceed the terms of a license, and you have gained the written permission of Cambridge University Press;
(iii) where you are allowed to reproduce without permission under the provisions of Chapter 3 of the Copyright, Designs and Patents Act 1988, which covers, for example, the reproduction of short passages within certain types of educational anthology and reproduction for the purposes of setting examination questions.

Contents

Introduction ... 5

1 Different voices – different times ... 6
1. What is a prologue? ... 6
2. Delve into detail ... 8
3. Focus on technique ... 10
4. Write a short prologue ... 11
5. Meet the River Singers ... 12
6. Phrases and sentences ... 14
7. Review word classes ... 16
8. Review dialogue ... 18
9. Voices ... 20
10. Finding out about flashbacks ... 23
11. and 12 Create Voice 4 at the museum ... 24

2 People in the news ... 26
1. Making headlines ... 26
2. Read and make meaning ... 27
3. Go deeper ... 30
4. Make a point ... 31
5. Facts and opinion ... 33
6. Read an autobiography ... 35
7. Another life ... 37
8. Make a start ... 39
9. Others in the news ... 40
10. and 11 Making the news ... 43
12. Give a presentation ... 44

3 Poems – old and new ... 45
1. The River ... 45
2. The Brook ... 47
3. Look deeper ... 49
4. Comparing poems ... 51
5. The cataract ... 53
6. Plan a performance ... 56

4 Time passing ... 57
1. Looking into the future ... 57
2. Put yourself in their shoes ... 60
3. Useful punctuation ... 61
4. Begin planning a longer story ... 64
5. Going back and looking into the future ... 65
6. Working with voices and moods ... 68
7. Working with chapters, paragraphs and connectives ... 70
8. Write paragraphs describing fictional surroundings ... 72
9. Going back in time ... 72
10. Spelling, punctuation and structure challenge ... 74
11. Finish your story ... 76
12. Take part in a *Readaloudathon!* ... 76

5 Poles apart ... 77
1. Describe and compare ... 77
2. Summarise and write paragraphs ... 79
3. Analyse a news report ... 82
4. Have a discusssion ... 84
5. Keep it formal ... 86
6. Using the passive voice ... 86
7. Read and assess a balanced report ... 88
8. Language techniques ... 89
9. Write a balanced report ... 91

10 A biased view	92
11 Argue a case	93
12 Have a class debate	94

6 Words at play — 96
1 Poetic licence — 96
2 Compare poems — 98
3 Do sounds and letters always agree? — 101
4 Made-up words and nonsense — 103
5 Have fun with words — 105
6 Laugh with limericks — 106

7 A different medium — 109
1 All the world's a stage — 109
2 What has changed? — 112
3 Using language — 113
4 Shakespeare alive — 115
5 Introducing manga! — 117
6 Shion — 119
7 Standard format — 120
8 Medium makes a difference — 120
9 A multimedia novel — 121
10 Language matters — 124
11 Plan an episode — 126
12 Write and display a final copy — 127

8 Make it happen — 128
1 Weighing up waste — 128
2 Read a magazine article — 129
3 Compare texts — 132
4 Revise punctuation — 133
5 Follow instructions — 134
6 Use the command form — 136
7 Create your own design — 138
8 Read a non-chronological report — 139
9 Summarise the report — 142
10 and 11 Write a non-chronological report — 143
12 Create a group magazine — 144

9 Snapshot — 145
1 Fruit in a bowl — 145
2 Poetic form and features — 147
3 There for a moment — 148
4 Features for effect — 151
5 A jewel — 152
6 Try 'encapsulating' a snapshot — 155

Spelling activities — 156
Term 1 – Revise common spelling sounds; Recognising unstressed vowels; Prefixes can give clues to meaning; Suffixes can change the meaning of words; Tricky endings; Not wrong, just different

Term 2 – Revise common spelling sounds; Soft and hard *c* and *g*; Forming nouns from verbs; Working with opposite prefixes; Revise a spelling rule

Term 3 – Revise common spelling sounds; Choose precise words; Homophones and homographs; The prefix *ad*; Revise a spelling rule

Toolkit — 165
Presentation skills; Nuts and bolts of writing; Keeping a learning journal; Using an etymological dictionary; Unit 1: Listening text; Unit 2: Biography; Unit 3: Poems; Unit 5: How to have a debate; Unit 7: Book talk

Welcome to the *Cambridge Primary English* Series, Stage 6.

This Learner's Book takes you through Stage 6 of the Cambridge Primary curriculum. It contains nine units of lessons and activities to help you develop your reading, writing, speaking and listening. skills This book covers all the skills you need to develop in Stage 6.

Each term has two long units and one shorter one. Over the year you will work through three units on fiction and plays, three on non-fiction and three on poetry. The long units are divided into 12 sessions. Some sessions have been omitted to create longer working periods to suit the activities. Each unit has a theme full of interesting and relevant topics. You will read classic writers and poets alongside science fiction and stories that play with time. You will also have fun with reading in different media with a graphic novel, a Japanese manga comic book and a multimedia novel. You will express your preferences, engage in discussion and do some role play and performance. In non-fiction you will come across a wide range of text types, some of which you will have encountered before.

We hope that you enjoy the variety and feel confident at recognising the features of the various different text types, and that you will try your hand at them as you investigate, explore and enjoy the different ways we communicate and express ourselves.

You will work in a variety of ways, in groups, with a talk partner or on your own, and of course at other times your teacher will lead a discussion or explain an activity. You will need all of your reading skills and you will keep a learning journal to record, remember and give yourself practice at different texts and techniques.

Working together is important, so you will have plenty of opportunities to share ideas, build your confidence and learn from each other, as well as from your teacher and the course books.

These icons will show you how you're going to work:

 have a discussion

 do some reading

 do some writing

 role play, read out loud or do an oral activity

 do a spelling activity

You'll find some extra help along the way, so look out for these features:

Tip
These tips give you handy hints as you work.

I am here to give you reminders and plenty of ideas.

Did you know?
These boxes encourage you to think broadly and do further research.

How did I do?
These boxes ask you to evaluate how you are doing. Answer the questions honestly – there is no right or wrong answer.

Language focus
These boxes explain helpful language rules. You'll need to remember the information to use again.

On pages 156 to 164 you'll find helpful spelling rules and activities to practise and expand your knowledge of words and their spelling.

On pages 165 to 176 you'll find a handy set of resources you can use at any time, such as advice on sentences, paragraphs and connectives and how to use your learning journal or have a debate. You'll also find complete poems and a listening text. We hope you enjoy the course and that it helps you to feel confident about responding to English, and using English in a variety of ways.

Sally Burt and Debbie Ridgard

1 Different voices – different times

Have you ever described something only to have someone else say it didn't happen like that at all? Books let us experience action, adventures, dilemmas and dramas as characters or narrators tell their stories. In this unit you'll experience different voices telling their stories and create the voice of a character yourself.

Vocabulary to learn and use: prologue, preface, perspective, omniscient, ancient, portray, authentic, homograph, rumour, vole, weasel, heron

1 What is a prologue?

A When tales start with *Once upon a time*, we know what sort of story to expect. But what other techniques can be used to begin stories?

1 Read the first paragraph of a library book or your reading book.
   - Does it set a scene or introduce a character?
   - Does it leave you curious to know more?

2 Read this opening paragraph of a story.
   a What images set the scene?
   b What is the feeling in this opening paragraph?
   c Is the narrator looking forward or back? How can you tell?
   d What is your opinion of this opening? Does it make you want to read on?

The Middle of Nowhere

The piano arrived too late to stop the sky falling in. If it had come earlier, things might have ended on a sweet note. As it was, everything was jangled, unstrung, struck dumb.

Geraldine McCaughrean

B Some books begin with a prologue. Work with a talk partner.
1. Where do you think the prologue comes in a book?
2. What role could it play?
3. Does the prologue below match your ideas? How?

Language focus

The word *prologue* comes from an ancient Greek word, πρόλογος (prológos), which is made from *pro* ('before') and *lógos* ('word').

The River Singers

Prologue

The rumour spread from burrow to burrow down the length of the Great River. The females, eyeing each other over their boundaries, commented on it in hushed tones. The males spoke of it with raised chins and defiant looks, before moving on and away to their own business. The rumour told of a new danger to the Folk. It told of a horror which came in the night. It told of the Great River stripped bare of her people, of entire colonies gone. It told of the end of their world.

But perhaps, they thought, a rumour is all it was. The ancient enemies – the fox, heron, weasel – had always been there, awaiting the unwary or unlucky. And still the Folk prospered. The Great River sang, her grasses were plentiful, and her waters were warm and bustling with life. No, perhaps rumours were only rumours and the lives of the Folk would continue as before. But even so the mothers turned an eye to their young, and slept more lightly than they had. And the males scented the breeze more carefully before straying into the open, ran more quickly, fed more watchfully.

Sylvan and the others, nestling in their chamber, knew nothing of the rumours. They knew nothing of the outside. They knew their mother, the scents of their home, and the rhythms of the Great River. They knew hunger which could be quenched with milk. But one day they would learn that sometimes a rumour is more than a rumour. Sometimes a rumour is a life which has yet to come.

Tom Moorhouse

C Start a learning journal to record this year's reading, your ideas and writing techniques you encounter and want to remember.

1. Add *The River Singers* to your learning journal.
2. Make notes on what the prologue suggests about the story.
3. List any questions you have about the story.

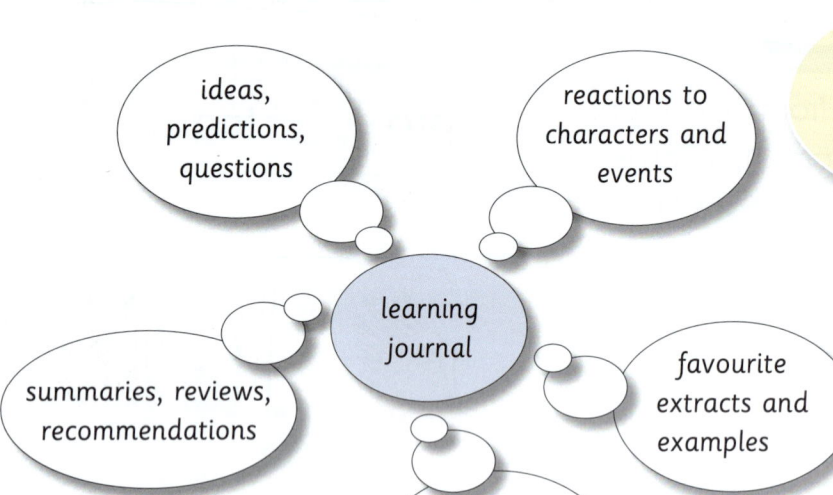

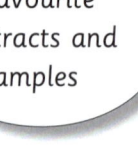

You can draw and stick things in your learning journal, and use it to practise your ideas.

2 Delve into detail

A The prologue for *The River Singers* contained important clues about the story to come. How many did you pick up?

1. Use these questions to find out how good a detective you are. Use evidence from the text in your answers.
   a. What clues show that the characters are not human?
   b. Who are the 'Folk'?
   c. What could the 'horror' be?
   d. What do you think is behind the rumour?
   e. Who lurks as 'ancient enemies'? Why are they 'ancient'?
   f. Are the Folk still wary? How can you tell?
   g. Why do Sylvan and the others know nothing of the rumours?
   h. What do the last two lines suggest about the rumours?

Tip

Look in more than one place for answers – scan the whole text for details that build up your ideas.

Unit 1 Different voices – different times

2. Choose a word to describe the mood of the prologue.

> suspense   tranquillity   foreboding   excitement
> menace   hilarity   anxiety

   a. Which words in the text support your choice?
   b. How could you change the mood of the prologue?

3. Summarise your predictions about the story in your learning journal. Note the genre and whether you might enjoy the book.

4. Which of these descriptions matches the prologue in *The River Singers*?
   - It is a flashback giving the readers clues to help them understand the story events and characters.
   - It is a 'flash forward' revealing later events to build suspense – foreshadowing.
   - It is spoken by an all-knowing narrator who gives hints of things the characters cannot know.

5. In your own words, explain what a prologue is and suggest why authors might use one.

How did I do?

- Did I find clues to answer the questions?
- Can I explain what a prologue is?

B Many words in English come from ancient Greek.

1. **Pro** has two meanings when it is used as a prefix. Which meaning fits each of these sentences?

   > **pro** *prefix* 1 before in time, place or order; 2 favouring or in support of

   a. I am very pro-homework because it helps me learn more!
   b. The aardvark has a prominent nose – it sticks right out.

2. *Logos* is Greek for 'word'. Many English words have the suffix **ology** or **logy**, meaning 'the study of'. For example, *biology* is the study of living things, because *bio* is Greek for 'life'.
   a. Tell a talk partner how the suffixes **ology** and **logy** could be related to *logos* meaning 'word'.
   b. Find and list words that end in **logy** or **ology**.

Session 2 Delve into detail

Did you know?

Some books have a preface where the author explains how the book came to be written. *Preface* comes from the Latin words *pre* ('before') and *fari* ('speak'). An etymological dictionary gives the origins of words. There's an example on page 169.

3 Focus on technique

A The *narrative voice* that authors choose helps them present characters and settings in a particular way.

1. The prologue of *The River Singers* is written in third person narrative. How can you tell? Discuss examples from the text.
2. Scan the prologue for clues about the type of narrator in the prologue.

Language focus

There are two types of third person narrative.
- The *third person narrator* tells the story from the outside but gives no information that the characters cannot know.
- The **omniscient** *third person narrator* tells the story from the outside but seems to know everything about the characters and events – past, present and future. It often gives clues and comments to the reader.

omniscient *adj.* having or seeming to have unlimited knowledge

B Sometimes authors write about things they feel strongly about, such as friendship, loyalty or protecting the environment.

1. Do you think you can tell from the prologue what the author of *The River Singers* feels strongly about?
2. Is the opinion of the author the same as the opinion of the narrator of the prologue? What makes you think this?
3. Should authors let their opinions and feelings come out in a book? Discuss your views.

Unit 1 Different voices – different times

C Repetition can make a point or create an atmosphere.
1. Which key word is repeated in the prologue? Why?
2. Do you find the repetition in the last paragraph effective? Why?
3. Practise describing something by using repetition followed by a contrast. Add it to your learning journal.

D Most of the prologue is in the same tense; but not all of it is.
1. What tense is it mainly in? Why is this tense often used in narrative?
2. Where and why does the tense change? What is the effect?

E Proper nouns have two important characteristics: they name specific (one of a kind) items and they always begin with a capital letter.
1. Is *folk* a common noun or a proper noun? Check in a dictionary.
2. Use *folk* in a sentence to show what it means.
3. Why does *Folk* have a capital letter in the prologue? How does this change its meaning?
4. Find and explain any other unusually capitalised words in the prologue.

4 Write a short prologue

- Flashback to much earlier events?
- Someone looking back long after the events?
- Different narrator perspective?
- Flash forward giving clues about the story?
- Something else?

- Type of book (genre)?
- First or third person narrative?
- Who is in it?
- What happens (summary)?

A Plan and write a prologue for your reading book. Ask yourself questions about your book using the suggestions in the picture on page 11.

1 Jot down notes on what your prologue will include.
2 Write a prologue of two or three paragraphs, using some of these techniques:
- repetition of key words or phrases
- carefully chosen words to create the mood you want
- clear narrative voice (third person or omniscient third person)
- consistent tense (only change it for dramatic effect)
- variety of short and long sentences.
3 Review your paragraphs for flow, check for errors, and make any improvements or corrections.
4 Swap prologues with a talk partner. Ask questions and make predictions about your partner's prologue. Did your partner pick up your clues?

> **Any volunteers?**
> I love prologues that give little hints and clues. Who would like to read out theirs?

5 Meet the River Singers

The River Singers

Chapter 1

Setting scene and introducing main character

The dawn was grey and the waters quiet. Sylvan was the first awake, lying with his brother and sisters in a pile of cosily intertwined limbs. Their breathing lulled him even as lightness spread up the tunnel and into the chamber, bringing with it the scent of the morning. He yawned. He opened his eyes. He grinned. Today was the day. At last.

Expanding on main character, giving clues about his personality

   Sylvan extracted himself, ignoring the others' sleepy protests, and sat with twitching whiskers at the entrance to the chamber. He should wait for them, he knew. They were supposed to go out all together. But the air stirred with a promise of new things and, with a final glance at his **siblings**, he stole away down the tunnel, paws padding on the soil. He had known the way for ages now. A left, a right, loop around a knot of roots, then pause at the place where the roof had fallen. One eye to the sky. Quiver. Listen. Check the scents. Then onwards and downwards to the lower places, the entrance to the Great River and the gateway to the world.

With each downward step the light grew brighter and the air fresher, more exhilarating. Another turn, a slight rise. And there she was: the Great River. Her waters, lapping against the family's trampled little platform, were bright through the shade of the tall grasses. She filled him with her vastness, her movement, her song. He felt the stirrings of hunger, the desire to dive, to twist, to flow with her. He hesitated, one forefoot raised, everything urging him out and into the world.

"And what exactly do you think you're doing, young vole?" A paw was on his tail, pinning it to the floor. Sylvan froze. He placed his foot hurriedly back onto the ground. As his mother removed her paw he turned, radiating guilt.

Tom Moorhouse

Explaining how strongly Sylvan is drawn to explore the river

A change of mood as Sylvan's mother interrupts

sibling *n.* a sister or a brother

Sylvan's journey

A The beginning of a novel often has a different mood and voice from the prologue.

1 Read the beginning of *The River Singers* aloud in a small group.
- As you read, identify the narrative voice.
- Does the voice seem the same as in the prologue?

2 **a** Choose words to describe the mood in the first paragraph.

> expectant sombre optimistic fearful buoyant light-hearted
> relaxed enthusiastic mischievous hopeful menacing humorous

b Find words and phrases in the passage that give clues.

Example: *cosily intertwined limbs – shows that they are relaxed, don't feel threatened and are not worried about sleeping*

3 Discuss how the idea of night becoming day helps to set the mood.

Session 5 Meet the River Singers

4 In one sentence, summarise the difference between the mood of Chapter 1 and the mood of the prologue.

5 Does this story opening match your predictions from reading the prologue? Give examples.

B **Work on your own before comparing answers with a talk partner.**
1. When do you find out what kind of animal Sylvan is? What were the clues?
2. What does Sylvan want to do?
3. Why do you think he is only supposed to go out with the rest of his family?
4. Describe in your own words how Sylvan feels about the river.
   Why might he feel this way?

C **The extract describes Sylvan's journey from his chamber to the edge of the Great River.**
1. Draw a sketch of the journey, including the details described.
2. Add captions to explain the features.
3. Use your sketch to retell Sylvan's journey to a talk partner.
   Compare your sketches and retellings.

> **Tip**
> Use time connectives, such as *first*, *second*, *after that*, *next* and *finally*.

How did I do?
- Did I retell a journey using my sketch and compare it with my talk partner's?
- Did I describe Sylvan's journey in the correct sequence?
- Did I use a variety of time connectives?

6 Phrases and sentences

A **Authors use a variety of sentence types to make their writing interesting.**
1. **a** In a group, discuss what makes a sentence. Develop a definition to share with the class.
   b Create a class definition to display on the wall.

Unit 1 Different voices – different times

2 Reorder the words in these sentences to make sense of them.
   a The fish caught a heron.
   b Underground dens live in foxes.
   c Adventure began his river in the Sylvan.
   d All their rivers lives in live fish.

3 Phrases are groups of words, without a verb, that go together to do a job. What could you add to turn each phrase into a sentence?
   a on the riverbank.
   b before his siblings.
   c beyond the burrow.

4 Choose a phrase from the box to add to the beginning and end of these sentences.

> **Tip**
> Sentences need a subject and a verb.

> at daybreak   on the riverbank   into the river   beyond the burrow
> after breakfast   with beady eyes   in the undergrowth   without his mother

   a The young voles ventured out.
   b The fox hid.
   c Sylvan did not explore.

B  **The author uses both phrases and sentences to describe Sylvan's journey, which is highlighted in the extract on page 13.**

1 Re-read each part of Sylvan's journey and with a talk partner decide whether it is a phrase or a sentence and say why. For example, *Quiver* is a very short sentence using the command form of the verb.

> **Tip**
> Command verbs are used for instructions and commands. You don't write the subject – it is implied: *(You) quiver.*

2 What is the effect of mixing phrases and sentences, both short and long? (Here's a hint – think about how a water vole would move.)

3 Write a short paragraph using a similar technique to describe the journey of another animal.
   - Think about how the animal moves.
   - Copy the pattern of phrases and one-word command sentences, choosing words that are suitable for your animal's style of movement.

Session 6 Phrases and sentences   15

- Swap your paragraph with a talk partner and suggest improvements. Use a thesaurus to help. Focus on verbs and freeze-frame your images.

C Scan the extract to find other descriptive passages which use a combination of long and short phrases and sentences.
- Write a few examples in your learning journal to remind you of the technique and note why you think it is effective.

7 Review word classes

A To form sentences you need words! It helps to be able to identify different word classes, and understand what they do and how they work.

1 Talk in a small group about the word classes in the box.
   a What does each word class do?
   b How can you identify each word class?

> noun   verb   adjective   adverb
> pronoun   preposition   conjunction

Tip
The different word classes are also known as parts of speech.

2 Look at the **Language focus** box and talk about how these pairs of sentences differ in meaning.
   a The water voles heard the rumour.
   b The water voles heard a rumour.
   c Sylvan ate a fish his mother had caught.
   d Sylvan ate the fish his mother had caught.

Language focus

Articles are the small words that come before nouns. They may be small but they make a big difference to meaning!

The **definite article** (*the*) refers to a specific noun.

For example: *Sylvan swam in the river.* (*a specific river previously mentioned*)

The **indefinite articles** (*a* and *an*) don't refer to specific nouns.

For example: *Sylvan swam in a river.* (*no particular river*)

Articles aren't always necessary with plural nouns.

For example: *Rivers are full of fish.*

3 Invent **five** sentences with this word class pattern.

> article + adjective + noun + verb + adverb
>
> The worrying rumour spread rapidly.

4 Discuss the word class of the underlined words.
   a My duvet is made of goose <u>down</u>.
   b The bird lined its nest with old <u>down</u> feathers.
   c An otter can <u>down</u> a whole fish in one go.
   d The heron looked <u>down</u> and spotted his prey.
   e The fisherman rowed <u>down</u> the river.

5 Choose three words from the box. Make up sentences using each word in at least two different word classes.

> well   light   round   like   work   walk   cook   present

B Words that look identical but have different meanings are called *homographs*.

Did you know?

Homographs may have different pronunciations. For example, the emphasis could go on a different syllable, as in **pre**sent (noun) but pre**sent** (verb). The word *homograph* originates from two ancient Greek words, *homós* meaning 'same' and *gráphō* meaning 'write'. Can you see why?

1 Use your dictionary to find the meanings of these homographs that also share a word class.
   a pupil (noun)
   b club (noun)
   c ring (noun)
   d bank (noun)
   e bat (noun)

2 Write pairs of sentences using the homographs in these word classes.
   a mean (adjective and verb)
   b watch (noun and verb)
   c minute (noun and adjective)
   d entrance (noun and verb)
   e content (noun and adjective)

3 Identify the word class of these words then use a thesaurus to find at least three synonyms for each one.
   a adventurous
   b disturb
   c warily
   d guardian

> **Tip**
> Synonyms have similar meanings, so they must be in the same word class.

8 Review dialogue

"Come on, Tiny. Mother's promised we're going out today."

Aven gasped and sat upright, pawing the sleep from her eyes. She groomed a little, setting her fur straight. She blinked her black eyes into focus.

"Sylvan," she said sweetly, "if you ever call me that again I'll gnaw your ears off."

Sylvan grinned, "You'll have to catch me first."

"Or wait until you're asleep."

He thought about it. "Good point," he conceded. "Can we go out now?"

Orris uncurled a little. "What's so good about going out, anyway?"

Sylvan sat back on his hind feet. "I don't know. It's just … better out there."

"Better?" said Orris. "Only if 'better' means 'full of weasels and owls and things that want to eat us'. I think I'll stay here."

"Mother said we're going out," said Sylvan, stubbornly.

"I hope you enjoy yourselves."

"Look," said Sylvan, "I'm the oldest and you need to do what I say."

"Says who?" said Aven.

Tom Moorhouse

A 📖 👥 **Authors use dialogue to show what characters are like through what they say and how they speak.**

1. In a group of three, read aloud the dialogue in this extract between Sylvan and his siblings, Aven (nicknamed Tiny) and Orris. Read one character each.
   - Scan the text to find and practise your words.
   - Use expression to show what your character is like.
   - Use actions to show the details in the narrator's words rather than reading them aloud.

   > **Tip**
   > Remember what you learned about Sylvan from your earlier reading.

2. From what you already know about Sylvan, does his conversation surprise you or does he act as you would expect? Why?
3. What does the dialogue reveal about the three characters?
   Draw a mind map for each one, noting:
   - whether they are a child, teenager or adult
   - five–six adjectives or phrases to describe them (e.g. *bossy, cheeky, fun-loving, nervous, lazy, sleepy, good at banter*)
   - any other relevant information.

   Remember, there are no right or wrong answers – it's *your* impression of the characters.
4. Perform the dialogue again, adding in your new understanding of the characters. Swap characters to see how different interpretations change the effect.

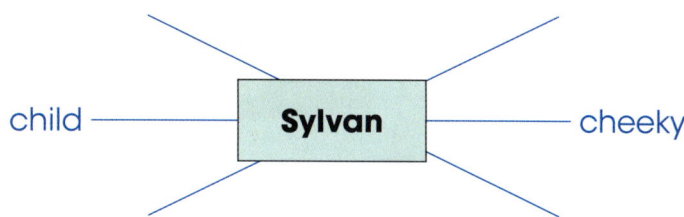

Session 8 Review dialogue

B ✎ **Revise your skills at dialogue and punctuation.**

"Sylvan," she said sweetly, "if you ever call me that again I'll gnaw your ears off." Sylvan grinned, "You'll have to catch me first."

With a talk partner, use this short extract to develop a memo to remind you of the rules for punctuating dialogue. Include these items in your memo:
- speech marks
- new line
- punctuation.

C ✎ **In your group, write more dialogue for the characters.**
1. Write dialogue in which Sylvan tries to persuade his siblings that it will be exciting to go and explore the Great River.
   - Make sure each character speaks at least twice more.
   - Focus on the verbs and words accompanying the dialogue.
   - Keep in character as you imagine what they say and how they say it.
   - Be imaginative – details make all the difference.
2. Give your dialogue to another group to perform and enjoy how they perform it!

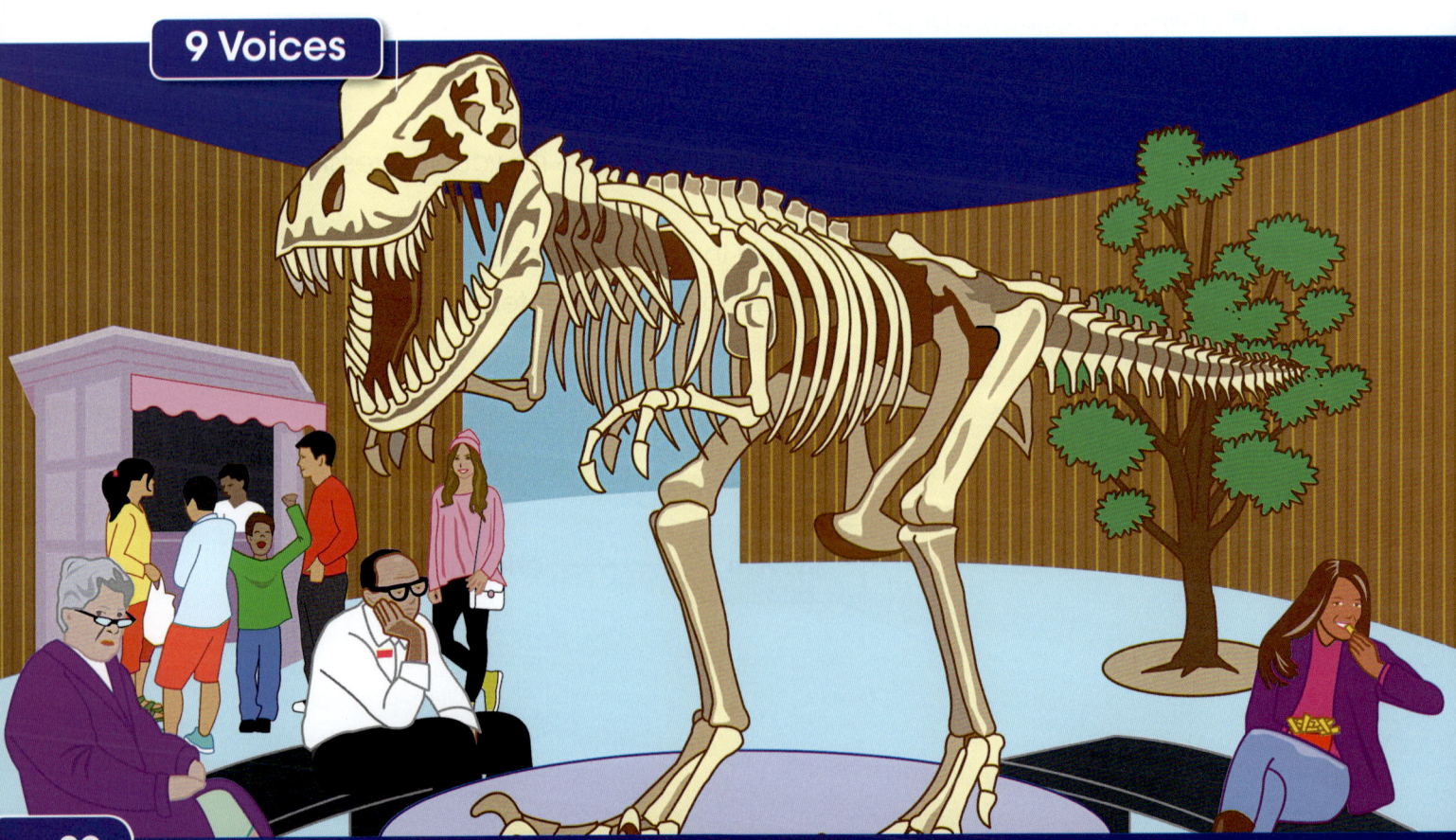

9 Voices

Unit 1 Different voices – different times

Voices in the Museum

Voice 1
It was time for our weekend educational outing. Maximilian dragged his heels as he always did on days like these; I can't think why. I believe a museum is most beneficial and improving. I always dress smartly on our outings, but my good coat is a little warm so I sat down on the bench in the Dinosaur Hall; you can see all the way down the hall from there, so I can keep an eye on Maximilian. That is the difficulty with weekends – so many people.

"Stay where I can see you," I warned. I wish that attendant had not sat down on my bench. I like my space and the other one was quite empty, if perhaps a little further away.

"Maximilian, this notice gives excellent information about Tyrannosaurus Rex." Is a bone missing just there? No. It must be my imagination. So much for education – Maximilian was nowhere near the replica dinosaur although I soon spied him further down the hall. I should have suspected he would find a food kiosk more interesting than the Jurassic era. Really!

Voice 2
Some people don't know how to sit – just sit. Like the lady on the other end of the bench. Fiddling about, buttoning her coat tight, fanning herself like crazy – craning her neck to see all over. Sitting's for relaxing, watching, thinking. I would've asked if she was OK but I was beat. Night shifts finish me but I like to be here waiting for young Jax when I come off shift. Wouldn't let her down. She loves that T-Rex. Knows every bone, she does, and has done since she was a nipper! Smart cookie she is. Reckoned I'd just put up with Miss Fidgety till Jax came with me coffee.

Voice 3
Poor Dad, he was sooooo tired, but we <u>always</u> do the dinos after his night shift – I think it cheers him up. I was getting him a coffee at the kiosk when this boy joined the queue, bouncing up and down all around me; he kept looking nervously over at this lady in a purple woollen coat sitting near Dad on the Dino Bench. She must have been sweltering – didn't she look outside this morning? For a moment I thought something was odd about the T-Rex but the boy was getting ON MY NERVES with all his bobbing about so I was distracted and forgot what I'd seen.

"You up for a cool drink, then?" I said. He cast another quick glance at *The Purple Coat*; then grinned and nodded. That broke the ice and we got chatting. He was a laugh, with loads of jokes and silly voices – just the way I imagine a younger brother would be if I had one. We'd just got to the front of the queue when I spotted *The Purple Coat* bustling our way …

A Not all stories are told as they unfold, from beginning to end.
1. By yourself, skim over *Voices in the Museum* to get the main idea.
2. In a group of three, summarise one 'voice' each in your own words to each other.
3. Read the story together, focusing on bringing out your character.

B Each character looks back on the same events, yet they remember them differently. What you remember depends on your point of view.
1. Piece together the events from all the voices in a timeline.

Purple coat arrives

Dad comes off shift

2. What is each character like? Find clues in the text.

> **Tip**
> You can organise your answers in a table or use a method of your own.

	Sex	Age	What type of person?	Evidence from the text
Voice 1	Female	Adult		Voice 2 refers to her as a lady
Voice 2				
Voice 3				

3. Which voice appeals to you most? Why?

C Standard English is the correct, formal style used in books, newspapers, official documents and business. When we speak, we are not always so correct or so formal. Idiomatic expressions and contractions are part of everyday colloquial speech.
1. Discuss the non-Standard English in these sentences. Then rewrite them in Standard English.
   a. I would've asked if she was OK but I was beat.
   b. Reckoned I'd just put up with Miss Fidgety till Jax came with me coffee.

c Knows every bone, she does, and has done since she was a nipper!
   d You up for a cool drink, then?

D Characters are partly portrayed by how they speak.
   1 Which voice uses the most Standard English? Does it fit what you have learned about the characters so far?
   2 Re-read Voice 2, then role play the events in Standard English. How does it change the character?
   3 What do the way Voice 3 speaks, the punctuation and the text effects show about her? Describe her to each other.

10 Finding out about flashbacks

A A flashback is a story-telling technique where the author interrupts the main story to go back to events that happened earlier. Flashbacks can be the narrator's memories or separate events, but they always tell the reader something important connected with the main story.
   1 Have you had a flashback experience – a sudden vivid memory of a conversation or event? Talk about your experiences as a class.

B Develop your listening skills by using all your senses as you listen for detail.

Oliver Strange and the Journey to the Swamps

by Dianne Hofmeyr

Oliver has flown to Africa to find his scientist father. The minute he lands in Zimbabwe nothing goes according to plan. Before he knows it he is on a bus to Victoria Falls with a girl called Zinzi and a bushbaby called Bobo.

1 Listen to an extract from a novel that uses a flashback. First read the title and snippet to give you some context, then jot down notes to answer these questions as you listen.
   a Where is Oliver at the start of the extract?
   b What strange things have happened?
   c Where and when is the flashback set? Who is Oliver with?
   d Which countries has his father visited? Why?

2 On a large sheet of card, draw up a timeline of the story events so far. What comes first?

11 and 12 Create Voice 4 at the museum

A In *Voices in the Museum* (on page 21), three characters narrated the events but a fourth person was also part of the story. Work in groups.

1 Build a profile of Voice 4 using these questions. Search for evidence from the other voices.
   a Who is Voice 4? How is he linked with the other characters?
   b Did he want to go to the museum? How do you know?
   c What did he do and whom did he meet?
   d Why did he keep glancing at the woman in the purple coat?

2 Take turns to role play Voice 1, 2 or 3, saying what 'you' think about the other characters.

   Example: I'm the man on the bench. That cheeky boy bobbing about in the queue makes me laugh – he looks loads of fun.

3 Take turns to role play Voice 4 and say what he thinks about the events and the other characters.

B A few days after the museum visit, Voice 4 discovers a dinosaur bone under his bed that's been missing from the museum.

1 Imagine you are writing the story of *The Missing Dinosaur Bone*, in which Voice 4 gets into an adventure with Jax. In chapter 3 of the story, Voice 4 has a flashback to the museum visit. What clue could be in his flashback?
   - Write a draft of Voice 4 narrating his museum flashback.
   - Write from his point of view in the first person.

- Start with the words: *Now I was really in trouble – how could I explain the dinosaur bone under my bed? It all started last week at the visit to the museum.*
  "What are you doing up there?" Gran called. ...

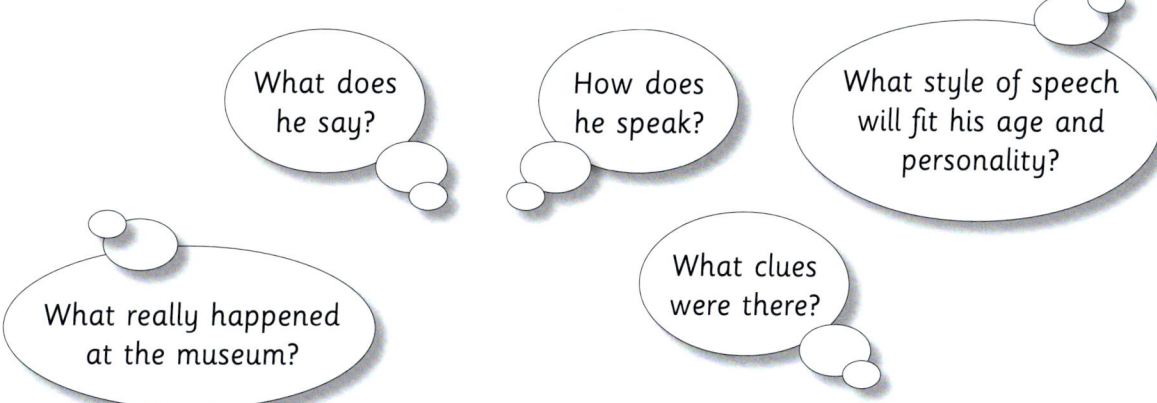

2. Ask a talk partner to read out your draft. Listen carefully.
   - Does your version of events fit with the other voices?
   - Does the boy's 'voice' sound convincing and **authentic**?
   - Did you include a clue that could relate to his adventure?
   - Does it make you want to read the story he is flashing back from?

   authentic *adj.* real or true; worthy of believing

3. Make improvements to your work. Focus on achieving a consistent voice and building suspense to draw your reader in.

   Tip

   Try using a mixture of sentences and phrases, and Standard and non-Standard English – put yourself in his shoes!

4. Enjoy reading your flashbacks to each other in a group. How differently did you all 'see' the events?

Session 11 and 12 Create Voice 4 at the museum

2 People in the news

In this unit you'll find out about people who have made headlines and shaped history. You'll investigate the style and language of a newspaper, an autobiography and a biography, plan your own autobiography and write an article about an unsolved mystery.

Vocabulary to learn and use: headline, article, lead, autobiography, obituary, chronological

1 Making headlines

A Different daily events make the news.
- Do you know the latest news?
- Do you read the newspaper? Why?
- What news topics interest you?
- What role does the news play in our lives?

B A headline is a main feature of a newspaper.
1 Skim over these headlines. Which one gets your attention first? Why?
2 Can you tell which news is 'good news'?
3 What is the purpose of a headline?

Bad weather STRIKES

And the winner is …

Rescue (mum) hero

Congrats – It's a boy!

'Unsinkable' liner goes down

Balloon trip: a great success

New mobile device 'a win'

Teachers, parents get A+

Unit 2 People in the news

C Headlines get your attention and send a message.

1. What is the effect of the punctuation marks in each headline?
2. What colloquial expressions can you find?
3. Choose **one** headline and rewrite it as a complete sentence. How does this change the headline? Is it as effective?

> **Tip**
> Use correct punctuation and have a subject and verb!

4. Make up a headline based on each of these sentences.
   a. Yesterday's match was cancelled due to the bad weather.
   b. The school tuck shop has changed its menu.
   c. The soccer team won their final match of the season.

Language focus

Different sentence types have different purposes:
- **statements** – state facts
- **questions** – require an answer
- **commands** – give an order.

An exclamation mark can be used at the end of a statement or command to express a strong feeling or emotion.

2 Read and make meaning

A Skim over the headline and first sentence of each paragraph in the article on the next page. Discuss the questions using the words *I think … because …*

1. What is the article about?
2. When and where did the event take place?
3. Is this news **current**?
4. Choose a word to describe the headline.

current *adj.* relating to the present time

> encouraging   inflammatory   disturbing
> outdated   relevant   interesting

Alabama News　　　　　　　　　　　　　　　**2nd December 1955**

Black woman arrested on bus

Yesterday, a black woman was arrested on a Montgomery bus, for refusing to relinquish her seat to a white passenger. Two policemen were called to the scene by the bus driver, who accused the woman of being disorderly and defiant.

Rosa Parks, a 42-year-old seamstress at a local department store, boarded the bus after work last evening and sat in the section reserved for black passengers, as required by the segregation law in Alabama. When the white section of the bus filled up, the driver, Mr James Blake, demanded that she vacate her seat. Mrs Parks, who claims she was tired after a day at work, refused to move. The driver called the policemen, who arrested her and removed her.

Mrs Parks, a senior member of the local branch of the National Association for the Advancement of Colored People (NAACP), is no stranger to public attention. She and her husband Raymond, also a member of the NAACP, are both active in helping black

people to register to vote and have taken part in numerous protests against the segregation laws. Previously, she was thrown off a bus when she refused to use the back door (the door black passengers are required to use).

Mrs Parks's court appearance will take place on Monday when she will be charged with disorderly conduct and defying segregation law. Members of the colored community have called for a bus boycott in protest at her arrest.

B 　　　Read through the news report in detail on your own.

1 Try to work out the meaning of any unfamiliar words from the context and jot down your ideas in your notebook. Check the meanings in a dictionary. Were you right?

2 What is a *department store*? What other words can be used? What word do you use?

3 Are there any other words in the report that are different from the words you use or are spelled differently?

4 What is the correct term for using initial letters of words as a short name for something e.g. NAACP?

C ✎ **Write answers to these questions in your notebook.**
1. What did Rosa Parks do for a living?
2. Why was she arrested?
3. Was this her first offence?
4. What were her reasons for her behaviour according to the report?
5. What punishment did she face?
6. Summarise the main idea of each paragraph as a headline.
   Example: Paragraph 1 – Woman arrested on bus

   > **Tip**
   > A summary is a brief version. It must be written in your own words.

7. Many years later, Rosa Parks said: "The real reason of my not standing up was I felt that I had a right to be treated as any other passenger." Judging by this statement, do you think the report was accurate in every detail? Why?

D 💬 **Have a group discussion.**
1. Talk about these questions.
   - Did Rosa Parks do anything wrong? Did she deserve to be arrested?
   - What would you have done in her situation?
   - Should young people give up their seats in public places for older people?
2. Summarise the group's responses using some of the words below, and choose a spokesperson to report back to the class.

   > Some members of our group feel that … while others believe …
   > Some say … but others think …
   > The group agrees that … because …
   > Most of the group say … However, a few say …

3 Go deeper

A **The style** is the way in which a text is written. The style should fit the purpose and audience. Make notes in a table like the one shown here to analyse the purpose and style of the report.

Purpose	Language	Style	Impact	Format

1 What is the intended purpose of the news report about Rosa Parks?
 - a to entertain children
 - b to inform the public
 - c to advertise something
 - d to interest people

2 Does the news report use correct, Standard English or informal language with colloquial expressions? Why?

3 How would you describe the style of the report? Choose one or two words from the box.

> personal   impersonal   formal   friendly   serious   chatty

4 What impact do you think this article had on its readers at the time? Do you think it would have been a positive or a negative reaction?

5 How is the news report organised? How does its format help the reader?

6 Make notes in the table of any other thoughts you have about the report.

Did you know?

The Rosa Parks story has become one of the most well-known events in history. Her arrest eventually led to the end of racial discrimination in public places in the USA.

B Which **proverb** best sums up the Rosa Parks story? Explain your choice.

1. There is strength in numbers.
2. Actions speak louder than words.
3. It's better to be remembered for standing out in a crowd than to be forgotten for blending in.
4. If you go against the grain you may get splinters.

> **proverb** *n.* a short sentence, usually known by many people, stating something commonly experienced or giving advice

C Look out for other articles about people in the news and add them to your learning journal.

4 Make a point

A A **journalist** has to decide which details to include in an article and what to say first.

> **journalist** *n.* a person who writes for a newspaper

Yesterday, a black woman was arrested on a Montgomery bus, for refusing to relinquish her seat to a white passenger. Two policemen were called to the scene by the bus driver, who accused the woman of being disorderly and defiant.

Language focus

The **lead** is the first sentence or two of a news report. It provides the most important details – who, what, when, where, why and how – and draws the reader in. The rest of the report gives extra details, quotations and opinions about the event.

1. What details does the lead of the Rosa Parks report give?

Any volunteers?
Which questions have been answered – who, what, when, where, why, how?

2 Why do you think the following details were left out of the lead?

> She was returning from work.
> She was tired after a long day at work.
> She travelled home on the bus every day.
> She had no previous criminal record.

3 The structure of a news report is often described by journalists as an *inverted pyramid*, like this:

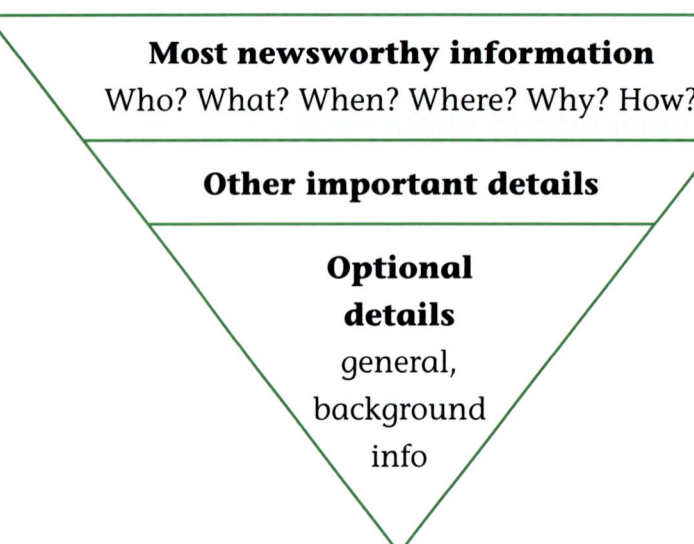

a In what order does the information flow?
b Why is it in the shape of a pyramid and not something else, like a rectangle?
c Draw the pyramid outline in your notebook, leaving space to write notes inside each section.
d With a talk partner, talk about where the details from the Rosa Parks news report fit into the pyramid.

Tip

Think about how important the information is, not about how much information there is.

B Plan a news report about an event that has occurred recently in your community.

1 Use the inverted pyramid to make notes about the event.
2 Write a headline and the lead paragraph only.
3 Edit and correct your work before writing it out neatly.

4 Display your work. Did everyone include answers to the *Who? What? When? Where? Why?* and *How?* questions in their lead?

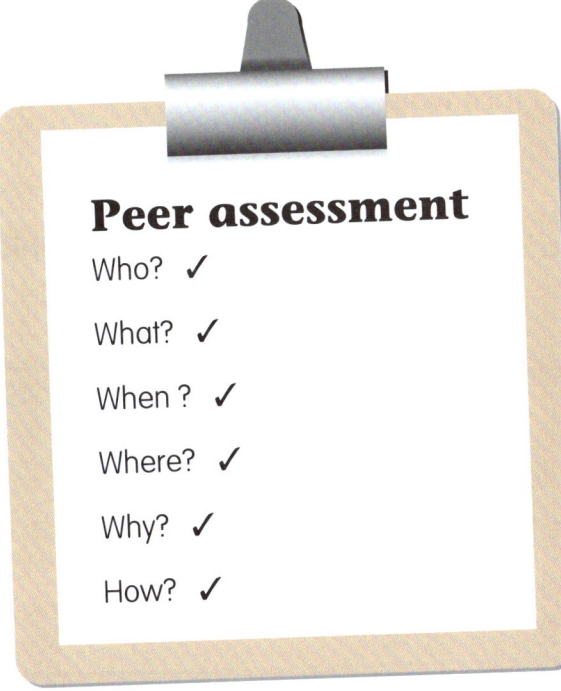

Peer assessment

Who? ✓

What? ✓

When? ✓

Where? ✓

Why? ✓

How? ✓

How did I do?
- Did I summarise events in headlines?
- Did I identify the key features of a news report?
- Did I write the lead paragraph of a news report?

5 Facts and opinion

A A news report gives the facts about an event and may also include opinions. Discuss the following in groups.

1. Why is it important that a news report has mainly facts?
2. How can you tell the difference between a fact and an opinion?

Language focus

A fact is a statement that can be proved. An opinion is based on someone's personal view.

The bus driver removed Mrs Parks from the bus is a fact – it can be confirmed by everyone there.

The bus driver was impolite is an opinion – some people might agree; others might disagree.

Session 4 Facts and opinion

3 Which statements are facts and which are opinions?
   a Mrs Parks was tired after a hard day's work.
   b She broke the law and was arrested.
   c The driver asked Mrs Parks to give up her seat.
   d She didn't deserve to be treated that way.
4 Write two facts and two opinions about any topic at your school.

B Vocabulary affects the tone of a story and can make an opinion sound like a fact.

Language focus

The **tone** is the way the writer expresses feelings, attitudes and emotions through choice of vocabulary, sentence length and punctuation. The tone may be described as angry, or bitter, friendly, humorous, concerned, judgemental, condescending, humble or enthusiastic.

> Previously, she was thrown off a bus when she refused to use the back door …

1 Which definition fits the word *thrown* in the article about Rosa Parks?

> **throw**, v.
> 1. to make something move through the air by pushing it out of your hand
> 2. to put something somewhere quickly without thinking about it
> 3. to make someone move or fall down suddenly
> 4. to make light or dark shapes appear on something

2 *She was thrown off a bus.* How would you describe the tone of this sentence?

> sharp   angry   sarcastic   friendly   humorous
> polite   insensitive   cruel   unkind   firm

Unit 2 People in the news

3 Choose different words to replace *thrown off* to make the tone of the sentence sound less emotive and more factual.

> pushed off   dragged off   escorted off   removed from

4 Use synonyms for the underlined verbs to change the tone to be less emotive.
   a She <u>refused to</u> give up her seat.
   b She <u>defied</u> the law.

Language focus

A verb describes the action or state of being of a noun or pronoun in the past, present or future tense. A news article reports an event in the past tense but may include a quote in the present or future tense.

5 Read the news report in Session 2 again, changing it into the future tense. What impact does this have? Complete this sentence in your notebook:

A news report about a past event is written in the past tense because ...

6 Read an autobiography

Chapter 1
How it all started

One evening in early December 1955 I was sitting in the front seat of the colored section of a bus in Montgomery, Alabama. The white people were sitting in the white section. More white people got on, and they filled up all the seats in the white section. When that happened, we black people were supposed to give up our
seats to the whites. But I didn't move. The white driver said, "Let me have those front seats." I didn't get up. I was tired of giving in to white people.
"I'm going to have you arrested," the driver said.
"You may do that," I answered.
Two white policemen came. I asked one of them, "Why do you all push us around?" He answered, "I don't know, but the law is the law and you're under arrest."

Rosa Parks

> **Did you know?**
>
> The word *autobiography* comes from the Greek words *auto* ('self' or 'by oneself'), *bio* ('life') and *graphy* ('writing').

A 📖 📝 **Years later, Rosa Parks published her story in an autobiography. Read the extract on the previous page and answer the questions in your notebook.**

1. Identify typical features of this type of text.
2. What similarities and differences are there between the news report about Rosa Parks on page 28 and the autobiography text?
3. Does Rosa Parks use Standard English or colloquial language to describe the event? Scan the text for examples.
4. What is the effect of the short, clear sentences?

5. What other details would you have liked to hear about?
6. Why do you think Rosa Parks began her autobiography at this point, instead of starting with her birth?
7. What else would you expect to read about in an autobiography?
8. Do you like reading about famous people? Why?

B 💬 **Discuss the differences between a news report and an autobiography.**

1. Who tells the story in each one?
2. What is the difference between you telling your story and someone else telling it? Who chooses the details?
3. If someone else wanted to tell your story, what style would you prefer them to use? Would you want them to include all the details or leave some out?

4   Tell a talk partner about something that has happened to you. Then take turns to tell a group your partner's story. How does it feel to have someone else relate your story? Did they get it right?

C Change these sentences from the third person to the first person by replacing the pronouns with the ones in the brackets.

Example: He did it himself. (I, myself). → *I did it myself.*

a   She wanted to sit by herself. (I, myself)
b   They were shocked by his actions. (we)
c   She decided to listen to him. (me)
d   They knew he was being unfair to her. (we)
e   She said she would leave by herself. (we, ourselves)

Language focus

When a sentence changes from third to first person, the pronouns change.
The first person pronouns are *I, me, we* and *us*.
Common third person pronouns are *he/him, she/her, it* and *they/them*.
Reflexive pronouns reflect back to a pronoun: *myself, yourself, himself, herself, itself, ourselves* and *themselves*. We use these to emphasise who did the action e.g. *I did it by myself*.

7 Another life

A Read and discuss an extract on the next page from an autobiography by Jamila Gavin, a well-known children's author.

1   Where and how does Jamila Gavin's autobiography begin?
2   Her story does not begin at the point when she was born. What effect does this have on the reader?
3   Is the beginning of her story attention-grabbing?

B Jamila Gavin's autobiography is set in a particular time in history.

1   What events were in the news when Jamila Gavin was a child?
2   Does she mention these events in the extract? What events does she mention?

Jamila Gavin's mother was English and her father Indian. Her autobiography describes her childhood in England and India during the Second World War (1939–45) and the struggle for Indian independence with the death of Mahatma Gandhi in 1948. She calls herself "a child of both countries and both cultures".

Chapter 1

Boasting

I used to boast about many things when I was a child, especially on the occasions that we came over to England from India – three times before I was eleven years old – and each time I had to start making friends all over again in a new school. So when I was asked questions about myself in the different school playgrounds I got to know, it would often go as follows:

Q: *"Where do you come from?"*
A: *"India."*
   I knew they thought of tigers and elephants and monkeys and fakirs sleeping on beds of nails.
Q: *"Where were you born?"*
A: *"In the Himalayas."*
   That impressed them. They imagined my mother giving birth to me on the icy slopes of Mount Everest some twenty-nine thousand feet up, when in fact I was born about six thousand feet up in the Community Hospital, Landour, Mussoorie which was in the foothills of the Himalayas.
Q: *"Have you ever seen a tiger?"*
   I may have been a boaster, but I wasn't a liar, and to this day I can't say that I have. But I still managed to make it sound glamorous and dangerous.
A: *"Not exactly, but I've seen its footprints in the mud and followed it all along the banks of the Brahmaputra River, and I've seen the long grass crushed where it has just lain, and I've seen the remains of its dinner still fresh, and known that it was not far away – maybe even watching us."*

3 Who was the author trying to impress? Why?
4 As a class, list any major news events you can remember happening in your lifetime and put them into chronological order.
5 What news events would you include in your autobiography? Why?

C **Autobiography is personal and can include facts and opinions.**
1 Identify three facts in the extract that are not based on the author's views.
2 Describe the author's thoughts and feelings about herself and her listeners.
3 When and why does the author use short sentences and long sentences? Who is she addressing?
4 In the last sentence, which connective is repeated many times? What is the effect?

D Add this autobiography to your learning journal. Note whose autobiography you would enjoy reading.

8 Make a start

A What would you put in your autobiography?
1 Make notes to plan your autobiography.
   a Where would you begin?
   b What details would be important?
   c What title and cover picture would you choose?

> **Tip**
> Remember that you don't have to begin at the beginning!

2 Plan and write the first paragraph only in no more than 100 words. Begin in an attention-grabbing way.
3 Swap paragraphs with a talk partner and get feedback on your paragraph. Check and edit your work.
4 Create your final version using neat handwriting or a computer.

B 🗨 **Have a discussion.**

1 When you write your autobiography, you choose what details to include. When someone else writes about you in a newspaper or book, they choose the details! Discuss how you feel about this, then choose a spokesperson to report back to the class.

> **Tip**
>
> Remember that connectives help to link ideas and make your speech flow smoothly. For example: "We think that … because … ." or "Our group agrees that … although … ."

2 What does this tell you about the things you read about other people?

How did I do?

- Did I identify what was fact and what was opinion?
- Did I analyse the key characteristics of an autobiography?
- Did I write the beginning of my autobiography?

9 Others in the news

Amelia Mary Earhart (born 24th July 1897, went missing 2nd July 1937, declared dead 5th January 1939)

After a long search, Amelia Earhart has been officially declared dead. Amelia Mary Earhart was an American aviation pioneer, author and women's rights activist.

She achieved a number of firsts in aviation history, becoming the first woman to fly solo across the Atlantic, the first woman to fly non-stop across the USA and the first woman to receive the Distinguished Flying Cross award. On 1st June 1937, Earhart and her navigator, co-pilot Fred Noonan, set off from Miami on an attempt to fly around the world. Their plane disappeared over the Pacific Ocean. Amelia Earhart will be remembered for her bravery, courage and pioneering spirit.

Frederick Joseph 'Fred' Noonan (born 4th April 1893, went missing 2nd July 1937, declared dead 20th June 1938)

Fred Noonan, who joined Amelia Earhart for the around-the-world flight as her navigator, has been declared dead. He was an American flight navigator, sea captain and aviation pioneer.

Noonan began his distinguished career as a seaman and officer on ships in World War I. He worked his way up to the rank of Master of large ocean-going vessels. Later he learned to fly and gained a reputation as an expert navigator. He charted many commercial airline routes across the Pacific Ocean during the 1930s.

On 2nd July 1937, he disappeared with Amelia Earhart somewhere over the Central Pacific Ocean during the last leg of their attempted around-the-world flight. His role in the development of commercial airline navigation earned him a place in aviation history.

A Read two **obituaries** and find out why these people are famous.

> **obituary** *n.* a report, especially in a newspaper, which gives the news of someone's death and details about their life

1. Are these texts similar or different? How?
2. Find examples of formal style: serious tone, title, topic sentence, conclusion, third person narrative.
3. What do the dates in the headings tell us?
4. In what ways were both people *aviation pioneers*?
5. Do you think the authors of these obituaries felt positive or negative about the people they were writing about? Describe the tone of each text.

Any volunteers? How is an obituary similar to a biography?

Session 9 Another life

B 🗨 📝 **Use parts of the verb *to be* as a linking verb.**

Language focus

The verb *to be* can link two nouns (or pronouns) or a noun (or pronoun) and an adjective.

noun (or pronoun) + noun (or pronoun):
  I **am** a pilot.   You **will be** a king.   We **were** children.

noun (or pronoun) + adjective:
  Ismail **is** famous.   She **will be** surprised.   They **were** happy

1 Use information from the obituaries to complete these sentences using nouns (or pronouns) or adjectives.
   a Amelia Earhart was a …
   b Fred Noonan was a …
   c They were …
   d Amelia is …

C 🗨 📝 **Express your opinion about an issue.**

1 Do you think that adventurers today are braver than adventurers of the past? Plan your response, then write a paragraph of no more than 80 words. Back up your ideas with facts.
2 Check and edit your work, then write it out neatly.
3 Take turns to read out your paragraphs. Did everyone agree?

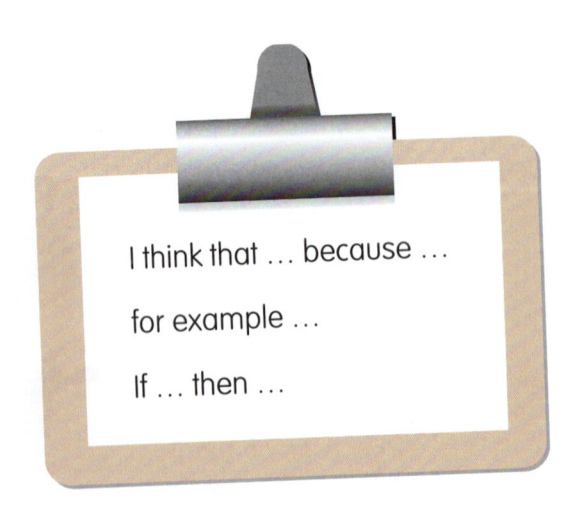

I think that … because …

for example …

If … then …

10 and 11 Making the news

Amelia lost!

Hopes fade of finding Earhart and Noonan

Search for Amelia called off

A 📖 📝 Plan and write a news report about the disappearance of Amelia Earhart and Fred Noonan.

1. Make notes from both the obituaries in the previous session to include in your report. Use the inverted pyramid on page 32 to order details from the most important to least important. You can find extra information in the timeline at the back of this book.
2. Write a first draft, including:
   - a lead that gives the most important details first
   - less important details in paragraphs 2 and 3
   - an eye-catching headline.
3. Check and edit your work, then create your final version using ICT or neat handwriting.
4. Create a class display or scrapbook of your news reports.

12 Give a presentation

A **Present a speech for two to three minutes.**

1 Choose a topic and set out your ideas under three main headings, using key words only.

> Things I'd like to do one day to make positive news!

> An extraordinary person who's made good news.

Get the audience's attention — **Introduction** — State your topic and purpose

Make 3–4 points in a logical order — **Main body**

Summarise your topic clearly and decisively — **Conclusion** — Make a lasting impression!

2 Practise your speech to build up your confidence. You could use a picture, photograph or poster to help you.

3 When you're ready, present your speech to the class. Good luck!

Unit 2 People in the news

3 Poems – old and new

In this unit you'll see how poets use words to create a timeless flow of water. You'll read poems by modern poets and poets writing more than a hundred years ago, whose words are just as fresh today.

Vocabulary to learn and use: brook, stream, cataract, grayling, surge, forget-me-not, eddy, recoil, critic, bitter

1 The River

A Rivers can be large or small.

1 Order these words for rivers from the largest to smallest, using the sound of the word and your prior knowledge to decide.

> river brook stream rivulet tributary torrent
> cataract burn rill streamlet beck runnel

2 Compare answers with a talk partner and check them in a dictionary.

B In pairs, read this poem by Sara Teasdale.

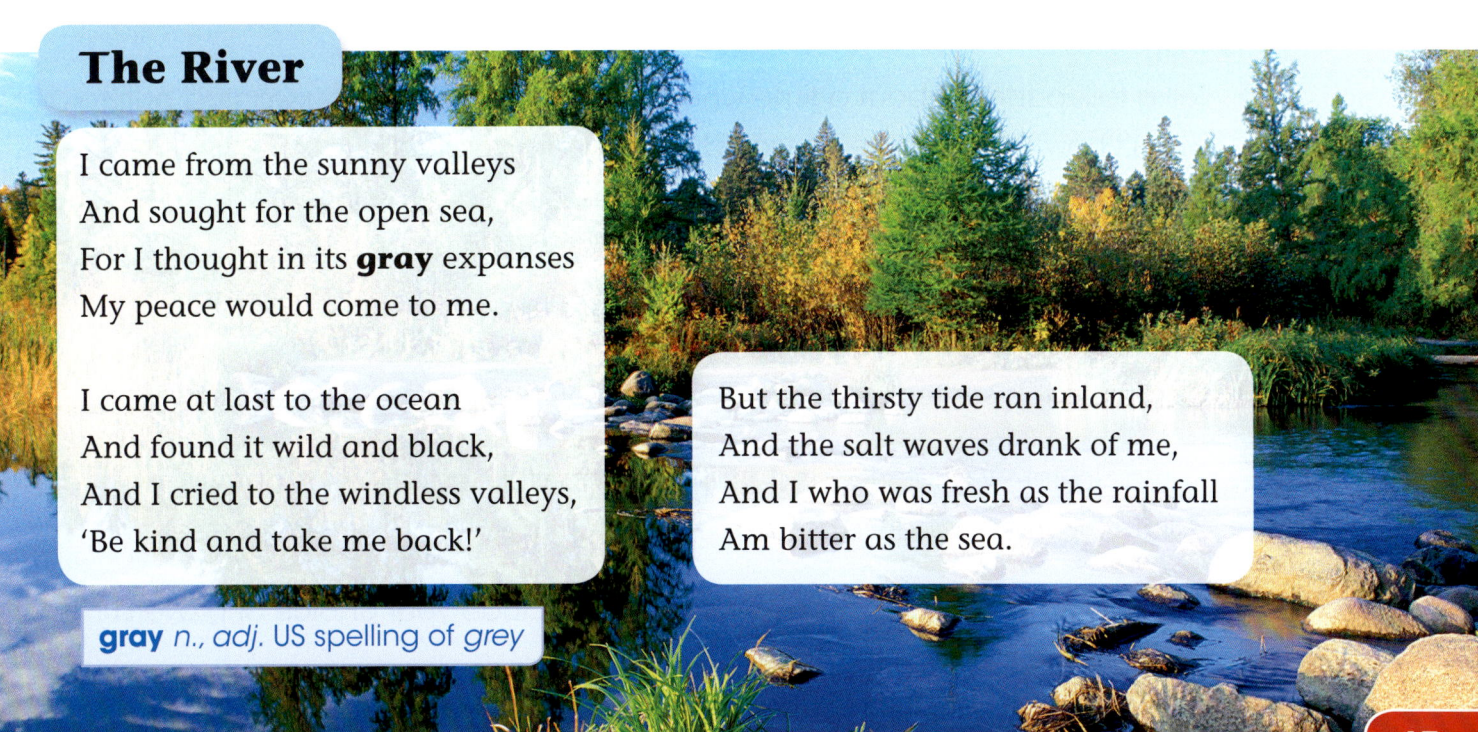

The River

I came from the sunny valleys
And sought for the open sea,
For I thought in its **gray** expanses
My peace would come to me.

I came at last to the ocean
And found it wild and black,
And I cried to the windless valleys,
'Be kind and take me back!'

But the thirsty tide ran inland,
And the salt waves drank of me,
And I who was fresh as the rainfall
Am bitter as the sea.

gray *n., adj.* US spelling of *grey*

Session 1 The River

1 Discuss the questions, then write your answers.
   a Describe the poem's features: stanzas, lines and rhyme scheme.
   b Who narrates the poem?
   c Summarise the poem's main idea in a sentence.
   d Where is the river's source?
   e What was the river seeking? Why?
   f How did the river react when it arrived?
2 a Write a sentence comparing the taste of seawater (or salty water) with fresh water.
   b Which definition of *bitter* best fits the context in the last line?
   c Why do you think the poet chose this word rather than *salty*?

bitter, *adj.*
1. angry and unhappy because of bad things you cannot forget
2. full of hate or anger: a bitter row
3. tasting unpleasantly sharp
4. painfully cold
5. causing deep pain: a bitter disappointment

Did you know?
Sara Teasdale was born in the USA in 1884 in St Louis, Missouri, which stands on the Mississippi, one of the world's longest rivers.

The poem describes the river's reaction when it finally achieves its wish.

1 Tell a talk partner about a time when you got something you wanted but it wasn't how you imagined it would be. How did you feel?
2 What do these proverbs mean? Which one best suits the poem's theme?
   - Grass is always greener on the other side of the fence.
   - All that glitters is not gold.
   - Pride comes before a fall.
3 Complete this sentence: *I think the mood of the poem is … because …*

joyful   wistful   jocund   bitter   sorrowful   carefree   mournful
light-hearted   angry   pensive   regretful   irreverent   solemn   resentful

4 Add *The River* to your learning journal and include your choice of proverb to explain its theme.

Unit 3 Poems – old and new

2 The Brook

A Alfred Lord Tennyson (1809–92) is a classic English poet. *The Brook* is one of his most famous poems.

The Brook

I come from **haunts** of **coot** and **hern**,
I make a sudden **sally**
And sparkle out among the fern,
To **bicker** down a valley.

By thirty hills I hurry down,
Or slip between the ridges,
By twenty **thorpes**, a little town,
And half a hundred bridges.

I chatter over stony ways,
In little sharps and trebles,
I bubble into **eddying** bays,
I babble on the pebbles

I chatter, chatter, as I flow
To join the brimming river;
For men may come and men may go,
But I go on forever.

I wind about, and in and out,
With here a blossom sailing,
And here and there a **lusty trout**,
And here and there a **grayling**.

I steal by lawns and grassy plots,
I slide by hazel covers;
I move the sweet **forget-me-nots**
That grow for happy lovers.

I slip, I slide, I gloom, I glance,
Among my skimming swallows;
I make the netted sunbeams dance
Against my sandy shallows.

And out again I curve and flow
To join the brimming river;
For men may come and men may go,
But I go on forever.

Alfred Tennyson

---

haunt *n.* a place often visited
coot *n.* a small, dark bird that lives near rivers and lakes
hern *n.* a heron, a type of water bird
sally *n.* a sudden or unexpected movement out from somewhere
bicker *v.* (of water) flow or fall with a gentle, repetitive noise; patter
thorpe *n.* small village

eddying *adj.* moving fast in a circle; swirling
lusty *adj.* healthy, energetic, and full of strength and power
trout *n.* a type of freshwater fish
grayling *n.* a type of freshwater fish
forget-me-not *n.* a small plant with blue flowers

1. In pairs, read the extract from *The Brook* on page 47.
2. Look up *brook* in your dictionary to find out its meaning as a verb. Use it as a verb in a sentence.
3. Choose three new words from the poem you would like to use again.
4. Share your words with another pair and experiment by using them in sentences. Add them to your word list.
5. Write a short paragraph describing a brook in your own words. Think about its size, the landscape it passes through, how it flows and where it is going.

B Many poems need to be read aloud to be appreciated fully.

1. Practise reading the poem aloud with a talk partner using the performance notes to guide you.
2. Experiment with different moods for the poem by varying the way you read it. What mood suits it best?
3. Perform your poem for another pair or group.

> Performance notes
> - Count the syllables in each line. What is the pattern?
> - Focus on rhythm, noticing stressed and unstressed syllables:
>   I COME from HAUNTS of COOT and HERN
> - Emphasise onomatopoeic words.
> - Think about your volume, pace and enunciation (how clearly you say each word).

Did you know?

An **iamb** is a unit of rhythm in a poem, consisting of an unstressed syllable followed by a stressed syllable (tee-TUM). This poem has four iambs in every other line.

3 Look deeper

A 💬 **Talk about these questions as a class.**

1. In stanza 2, the brook passes some things. Do you think the numbers are exact? Why?
2. Put the following extracts into your own words:

> I make a sudden sally
> And sparkle out among the fern,
> To bicker down a valley.

Tip

Don't forget to use the glossary!

Example: *I burst out bubbling through the ferns, to patter down the valley.*

a I chatter over stony ways,
In little sharps and trebles,

b I bubble into eddying bays,
I babble on the pebbles

B 💬 📝 **The poet uses poetic devices (figures of speech) to make the reader see, feel, hear and enjoy the brook's journey. Work with a talk partner.**

1. Describe the rhyme scheme, using letters (e.g. AABB).
2. In your notebook, list examples of onomatopoeia and alliteration.

Onomatopoeia	Alliteration
babble	sudden sally

Language focus

Rhymes at the end of lines are called **end rhymes**.
Rhymes in the middle of a line are called **internal rhymes**.
Words that almost rhyme are called **half-rhymes**.
Onomatopoeia means words that sound like the noises they refer to.
Alliteration is the use of several words that begin with same sound.

3 Is the narrator's voice the same as the author's? How can you tell?

4 Is the narrative voice an example of simile, metaphor or personification? Explain how you know using examples from the poem.

> **Tip**
>
> Look carefully at the verbs – which ones sound more like something *you* could do rather than a river?

5 What is your favourite image the brook sees during its journey? Tell your talk partner why you like it.

6 Imagine you are the brook. Write a vivid description of something else you see on the way and add a couple of lines to the poem.

7 Sketch the brook's journey, showing details from the poem.

C Talk as a class about the poem's themes and find its deeper meaning.

1 What is the message in the poem's repeated lines?

2 How does the tense emphasise the message? Give examples.

3 Which of these statements suit the deeper meaning in this poem? Use different parts of the poem to answer.

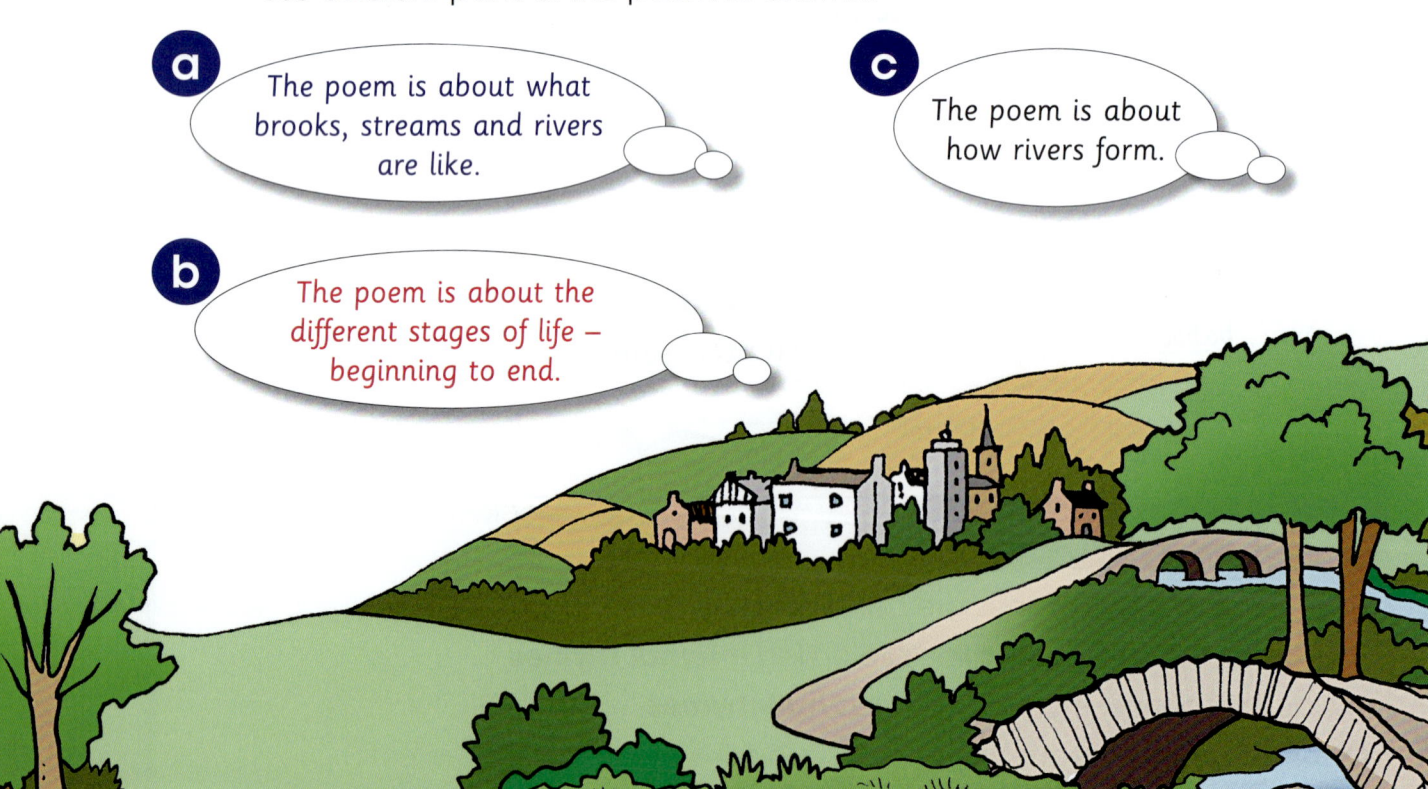

a The poem is about what brooks, streams and rivers are like.

b The poem is about the different stages of life – beginning to end.

c The poem is about how rivers form.

4 Comparing poems

A 📖 💬 👥 *The Brook* and *The River* are both classic poems describing water on a journey. The poems share similarities but the effect is very different.

1. Prepare a group presentation comparing the poems, using the *Critic's choice* leaflet.
2. Present to another group, who will score you against the criteria.

Critic's choice

Give a five-minute presentation comparing *The Brook* and *The River*. Use plenty of examples and liven up your presentation by performing extracts.

What do we need to talk about for each poem?
- ✓ Main idea and underlying meaning (2 marks)
- ✓ Structure: stanzas, length, rhyme scheme, rhythm, layout (2 marks)
- ✓ Narrative voice and mood (2 marks)
- ✓ Imagery or poetic devices: e.g. word choice, alliteration, onomatopoeia, personification (2 marks)
- ✓ A personal response to each poem, giving our preference (2 marks)

B 📖 💬 **Read two poems by modern poets.**

1. In pairs, silently read one poem each, thinking especially about the images and preparing to explain your poem to your talk partner.
   - Retell the story in your own words.
   - Say who narrates the poem and how you can tell.
   - Give examples of any poetic devices used: metaphor, simile or personification.
2. How does your poem compare with the other poems in this unit? Does it seem more modern than the others or is it just as timeless?

3 Explain your response to your poem. Did you enjoy it more or less than the others in this unit? Why?

Mawu of the Waters

I am Mawu of the waters.
With mountains as my footstool
and stars in my curls
I reach down to reap the waters with my fingers
and look! I cup lakes in my palms.
I fling oceans around me like a shawl
and am transformed
into a waterfall.
Springs flow through me
and spill rivers at my feet
as fresh streams surge
to make seas.

Abena P.A. Busia

Mawu a figure from ancient West African mythology

A River Poem

Inside the river are
the sky, the cloud, and the cold sun.
In my hands' bowl is the river.

If I throw up my hands,
the river spills in drops, scattering
sky, cloud, and sun all o'er me.

From my hands' bowl, if I drink
the river, then within me,
the sun, the cloud, and the sky.
Tell me, who is in who?

Mamta G. Sagar, translated by Chitra Panikkar with the poet

C Poetry is often set to music and movement to help interpret the words and create a dramatic performance.

1 How could you dramatise and interpret these poems with movement, gestures and body language? Have a go!

Any volunteers? Who can explain their poem to the class?

Tip
Be imaginative! Perhaps you could have different people being the different types of water coming to life as the narrator reads.

How did I do?
- Did I read a poem aloud with meaning and expression?
- Did I give my personal response to a poem?
- Did I compare poems?

5 The Cataract of Lodore

A Have you ever heard of a cataract? It has more than one meaning.

1 Predict which meaning of *cataract* is used in the poem *The Cataract of Lodore*:
   a a downpour of water; a deluge
   b a disease of the eye that gradually affects vision
   c a large waterfall.
2 Suggest a more usual synonym for *cataract*.
3 Read an extract from the poem aloud as a group.

The Cataract of Lodore

The cataract strong
Then plunges along,
Striking and raging
As if a war waging [...]
Sinking and creeping,
Swelling and sweeping,
Showering and springing,
Flying and flinging,
Writhing and ringing,
Eddying and whisking,
Spouting and frisking,
Turning and twisting,
Around and around [...]
And glittering and frittering,
And gathering and feathering,
And whitening and brightening,
And quivering and shivering,
And hurrying and scurrying,
And thundering and floundering;
Dividing and gliding and sliding,
And falling and brawling and sprawling,
And driving and riving and striving,
And sprinkling and twinkling and wrinkling,
And sounding and bounding and rounding,
And bubbling and troubling and doubling,
And grumbling and rumbling and tumbling,
And clattering and battering and shattering;
Retreating and beating and meeting and sheeting,
Delaying and straying and playing and spraying,
Advancing and prancing and glancing and dancing,
Recoiling, turmoiling and toiling and boiling,
And gleaming and streaming and steaming and beaming,
And rushing and flushing and brushing and gushing,
And flapping and rapping and clapping and slapping,
And curling and whirling and purling and twirling,

And thumping and plumping and bumping and jumping,
And dashing and flashing and splashing and clashing;
And so never ending, but always descending,
Sounds and motions for ever and ever are blending
All at once and all o'er, with a mighty uproar, –
And this way the water comes down at Lodore.

Robert Southey

B **Talk about the poem in a small group.**
1. Is the water flowing quickly or slowly? How can you tell?
2. Choose the best word to describe the poem's mood.

> melancholy   exuberant   wrathful   subdued   vengeful   boisterous

3. How does the shape made by the line lengths add to the poem?
4. How many full stops are there? What is the effect of reading it aloud?
5. Jot down five descriptive words you like. Explain why you like them.

C **The poet uses poetic techniques to create the waterfall effect. Choose three techniques and write a short paragraph on each.**
- a Start each paragraph with a topic sentence identifying the effect.
- b Explain how the technique works, including examples.
- c Give your opinion on how successful you think it is.

Language focus

Onomatopoeia, alliteration, repetition, rhythm and rhyme are all poetic techniques that use sound to help us imagine visual images.

D Add *The Cataract of Lodore* to your learning journal. Include your five favourite words and comment on whether you think the poet is a modern or a classic poet.

Session 5 The Cataract

6 Plan a performance

A All good storytellers use sounds, pauses, body language, an expressive voice and pace variation for dramatic effect.

1 *The Cataract of Lodore* is definitely meant to be read aloud! Plan a dramatic group presentation of the poem.
   - Decide what techniques you will use.
   - Plan who will say what: individually, in pairs and as a chorus. Make presentation notes to remind you.
   - Choose music and images to accompany your poem.

> **Tip**
> You could use ICT, sound equipment or make your own sound effects. Use props and your own sketches.

2 Practise your dramatic presentation and give each other feedback.
   a Mention three things that went well.
   b Suggest one thing that could be improved.
3 Perform your poem for an audience.

How did I do?
- Did I identify poetic techniques?
- Did I perform a poem?
- Did I add expression and use special effects?

If you'd like to read the complete versions of The Brook and The Cataract of Lodore, you'll find them on page 172 and 173!

Unit 3 Poems – old and new

4 Time passing

Writers have always enjoyed writing about time, space, the past and the future. In this unit you'll imagine travelling to another planet, to the centre of the Earth and back in time. You'll also write your own science fiction story.

Vocabulary to learn and use: voyage, ration, hue, mission, colony, empathise, brackets, titanic, vapours, geologist, science fiction, time travel, promontory

1 Looking into the future

A What will the future be like? What will be invented? Where in the universe might we go?

Did you know?

In 2013 over 200,000 people from more than 140 countries applied to be part of Mars One – a mission to establish the first human colony on Mars in 2024. The journey, estimated to take seven months, will be one-way only!

1. Would you apply to go and live on Mars? Share reasons.
2. What essentials might you need to start a colony on a planet?
3. Skim over the extract below. Where do you think the characters are going? What are they taking with them?

The Green Book

1. Father said, "We can take very little with us."
The list was in his hand. "Spade, saw, file, **ax**, for each family. Seeds, etc., will be provided. Iron rations will be provided. For each voyager a change of clothing, a pair of boots, *one or two* personal items *only*; e.g., a favorite cooking pan, a musical instrument (small and light), a picture (unframed). Nothing under this heading will be taken if it is bulky or heavy, fragile or perishable. One book per voyager."

Session 1 Looking into the future

2 It was easy to pack. We were allowed so little, and we didn't have to bother about leaving anything tidy behind us. Only the books caused a little delay. Father said, "I must take this." He showed us an ugly big volume called *A Dictionary of Intermediate Technology*. "But you must choose yourselves," he said. "It wouldn't be fair of me to choose for you. Think carefully."

3 We didn't think. We were excited, disturbed, and we hadn't really understood that everything else would be left behind. Father looked wistfully at the shelves. He picked up *The Oxford Complete Shakespeare*. "Have you all chosen your books?" he asked.

4 "Yes," we told him. He put the Shakespeare back.

5 We had time to waste at the end. We ate everything we could find.

6 "I don't want to eat iron," Pattie said, but nobody knew what she meant.

7 Then Father got out the slide projector, and showed us pictures of holidays we had once had. We didn't think much of them.

8 "Have they all gone brownish with age, Dad?" said Joe, our brother, the eldest of us.

9 "No," said Father. "The pictures are all right. It's the light that has changed. It's been getting colder and bluer now for years … but when I was young it was this lovely golden color, just like this – look."

10 But what he showed us – a beach, with a blue sea, and the mother we couldn't remember lying on a towel, reading a book – looked a funny **hue**, as though someone had brushed it over with a layer of treacle.

Jill Paton Walsh

ax *n.* American spelling of *axe*
hue *n.* colour

B Check your understanding in a group.

1 What clues show the story is set in the future?
2 Why do Father's pictures look wrong?
3 What do you find out about the characters? How do they feel?
4 How would you be feeling?

C This story opening gives clues about the upcoming journey.

1 a What is the root noun of the word *voyager*?
   b Find its dictionary definition to predict how far they are going.
   c Find synonyms for *voyage* in a thesaurus and discuss why the author chose to use *voyage* rather than a synonym.

2　a　Explain *rations* in your own words. When would you need them?
　　b　What are *iron rations*?
　　c　Why does Pattie say she doesn't want to eat iron? Why doesn't anyone know what she means?
3　Which meaning of *file* is in paragraph 1? How can you tell?
　　a　a collection of information and documents about someone or something
　　b　text, a picture or a computer program on a computer
　　c　a box or folded piece of thick paper to put documents in
　　d　a small tool with a rough edge to make a surface smooth
　　e　a line with one person following the other – single file
4　Use your answers so far and scan the text for further details to predict how long the characters are going for and why they are going.

D Revise ellipses and italics.

> ### Language focus
>
> An **ellipsis** (…) adds meaning in different ways.
> - It lets the reader imagine the missing details:
>   You had better finish your homework or else …
> - It builds suspense: Cautiously they opened the box …
> - It shows something has been omitted: "To be or not to be …" is the beginning of a famous Shakespearean quotation.

1　Italics are used to make words stand out for different reasons. Scan the extract for examples and explain why they were italicised.
2　What is the purpose of the ellipsis in paragraph 9?
3　Write three sentences to demonstrate the ellipsis used in each way. Share your sentences.

2 Put yourself in their shoes

A When we empathise with characters, we imagine what we would feel or do in their situation.

1 Why do you think Father chooses the book he does?
2 One child chooses *Robinson Crusoe*, a story about a man stranded on a desert island. Is this a good choice? Why?
3 What book and personal items would you take?
4 In pairs, spend one–two minutes preparing a short speech to explain your choices, and five minutes making notes. Then give your speech to a group, without using your notes.
5 In the next extract, why do Pattie's siblings laugh at her choice of book? What do you think of her choice?

Any volunteers? What is an impromptu speech?

It was thin and neat, with dark green silky boards covered with gold **tooling**. The edges of the pages were gilded and shiny. It had a creamy silk ribbon to mark the place, and pretty brown and white flowered end-papers. And it was quite empty.

"It's a commonplace book," said Joe. "A sort of jotter, notebook thing, for thoughts you want to keep."

tooling *n.* patterns imprinted using heated tools

B Some books introduce a key theme, or *golden thread*, which turns out to be important later on.

The voyagers need paper. Pattie's father asks her for her empty notebook.

"Heavens!" said Father. "What's this?" He read for a few moments. "It's a story," he said. "About here, about us. It has the moth people in it, and the hexagonal wheat!"

"Read it to us," said Jason's mother, and others joined in. "Read it to us!" Lots of people, the people of Shine, gathered around Father with the open book in his hand, all eager, and ready to make the words huge with listening to them. Father turned back and back in the green book to the very first page, and began to read:

"Father said, 'We can take very little with us'…"

> **Tip**
>
> When a speaker quotes someone else, another set of speech marks goes within the first set, either double marks within single, or the other way round:
> "Father said, 'We can take very little with us' ..."

1. Read the ending of *The Green Book* on page 60 with a talk partner.
2. What is familiar about the last line of the novel?
3. Use these questions to discover the 'golden thread' in this book:
   - What important item features at the beginning and at the end?
   - How is the novel's title significant?
4. What does this tell you about Pattie's book?

> **Did you know?**
>
> In ancient China people believed that when children were born, invisible red threads connected them with those who would be important in their lives, including people they had yet to meet. Can you see a link to the idea of a 'golden thread' in a novel?

C Add *The Green Book* to your learning journal. Add a comment explaining how its 'golden thread' worked.

3 Useful punctuation

A Brackets can be very useful in writing.

> **Language focus**
>
> Pairs of brackets, dashes or commas enclose a word or words to separate them from the main sentence. The bracketed words can be:
> - an explanation: Cairo (the capital city of Egypt) is near the Nile delta.
> - additional information: Mount Elbrus in Russia, at 5642 metres, is the highest mountain in Europe.
> - an aside or afterthought: I watched the match – which was brilliant – before going to bed.

1 Choose the best phrase to go inside the brackets in these sentences.

> not brown   the southernmost point on Earth
> previously called Constantinople
> the 2nd century BCE   or dromedary   gently

a The ancient Chinese invented paper during the Han Dynasty (…).
b Istanbul (…) is in Turkey.
c The South Pole (…) is on the continent of Antarctica.
d The camel (…) is well adapted for the desert.
e Cook the onions (…) until they are soft (…).

Tip

If you take away the bracketed words, the sentence should still make perfect sense.

2 Discuss how the brackets are used in paragraph 1 on page 57.
3 Scan the extract on pages 57 and 58 for examples of commas and dashes used as brackets.

B Focus on hyphens and dashes.

Language focus

A **hyphen** is a short line that links words together to create one idea:
X-ray, ten-year-old, sugar-free.
Dashes are longer than hyphens. A single dash can signal:
- a dramatic pause leading to a climax or anti-climax
- an aside or comment
- additional information or contrast.

She paused – then shouted, "Hurray!"

1 Use these hyphenated words in sentences of your own.

> T-shirt   bad-tempered   sports-mad   well-known   quick-thinking
> part-time   twenty-five   two-thirds   anti-clockwise

2. Talk about the role the dashes play in these sentences.
   a I was so hungry but lunch turned out to be – salad!
   b One twin had short hair – the other long hair.
   c My sister loves jogging – I think she's crazy.
   d We went up the hill – in a cart.
3. How is the single dash used in paragraph 9 on page 58?

C Colons can be used to introduce speech (especially in a play script), introduce a list or emphasise part of a sentence.

1. Write the following sentence in your notebook and add a list.

   If I had to go on a long journey, I would take:

2. Write a dialogue between Pattie and her brother when he discovers she has chosen an empty notebook.

   Pattie: What's wrong with my book?
   Joe: For a start ...

D In your learning journal, note examples of how brackets, dashes and ellipses are used for effect.

How did I do?

- Do I understand how to use brackets?
- Do I understand the difference between hyphens and dashes?
- Did I use punctuation to create effect?

4 Begin planning a longer story

A 📖 💬 Stories need to be planned carefully, especially if they are divided into chapters.

1 Chapters organise longer stories into episodes.

2 A new chapter starts:
- after the end of a series of events
- when there is a change of scene (like a play).

3 Chapters are like mini stories:
- the beginning sets the scene (and grabs attention)
- the middle describes the action and develops the storyline
- the ending wraps up the episode.

4 Chapters often end on a climax or leave you wondering about something to make you want to read on!

1. Read the information and summarise why chapters are important.
2. Analyse your independent reading books in a group.
   a. Do the chapters have a title, a number or both?
   b. Why don't all novels have a contents page?

B 💬 📝 In a group, plan an extended story.
1. In groups, suggest and discuss ideas for these criteria.

Criteria for science fiction
Readaloudathon!

- Moving to another planet – set in the future
- Items to take
- An item that will become 'important'
- The strange new environment
- An exciting climax or problem to be solved
- Dialogue and suspense
- Maybe a flashback or prologue?

2 Design a table to plan your story. Share your ideas.

Chapter	Episode plan	Paragraphs	Techniques
1	Introduce characters and what they are like Clues about why going to another planet Mention the special object		
2	Settling in (include something about object) Describe scenery Clues about upcoming problem		
3	A surprise discovery – special object or scenery leading to climax		
4	Conclusion – special object helps resolve the issue		

3 Plan the paragraphs for your first chapter. List any techniques you plan to use (e.g. ellipsis, italics, brackets).

4 Write a draft of your first chapter, starting with an attention-grabbing sentence. Leave it as a draft because you may want to add to it later when you carry on planning and writing your story.

5 Going back and looking into the future

A What did people 150 years ago imagine life would be like in the future? Are their ideas still science fiction or have they become old-fashioned?

1 What is science fiction? What are sci-fi (science fiction) stories about?

How are they different from fantasy?

2 Which of these stories sound like science fiction?

- Travelling in a time machine
- A story set in the year 2075
- A secret agent with impossible gadgets
- Discovering a lost city under the sea

3 Think of some things that had not been invented 150 years ago. Would people in those days think of them as science fiction?

B Read an extract from a classic 19th century science fiction book.

Did you know?

Jules Verne (1828–1905) was a French writer best known for his science fiction adventure novels – *A Journey into the Interior of the Earth, Twenty Thousand Leagues Under the Sea* and *Around the World in Eighty Days.* He wrote about space, air and underwater travel long before they became part of real life.

1 Jules Verne's writing style is very challenging because he was writing a long time ago. Read and discuss the extract in a group, using the glossary to help understand difficult words. Use context to predict the meaning of any other unfamiliar words before checking together in a dictionary.

2 What is the main idea of this extract on page 67 – is it to tell us more about the characters, or is it to create an impression of a different world? Use details from the text to answer.

3 How can you tell Axel's reaction to what he saw? What would your reaction be?

Unit 4 Time passing

4 How would you describe the scenery?

> fantastical   bizarre   magnificent   creepy   terrifying
> awe-inspiring   unpleasant   ugly   peaceful   menacing

5 Draw your impression of the forest of mushrooms.

Language changes over time.

Axel and his uncle, Professor Liedenbrock, are following in the footsteps of a geologist who claims to have travelled to the centre of the earth through a volcanic crater. They have come to an underground sea.

A Journey into the Interior of the Earth

Chapter 30: A new *mare internum* (inland sea)

[1] "Well, take my arm, Axel, and let us follow the windings of the shore."

[2] I eagerly accepted, and we began to coast along this new sea. On the left huge pyramids of rock, piled one upon another, produced a **prodigious titanic** effect. Down their sides flowed numberless waterfalls, which went on their way in brawling but **pellucid** streams. A few light vapours, leaping from rock to rock, marked the place of hot springs; and streams flowed softly down to the common basin, gliding down the gentle slopes with a softer murmur. …

[3] But at that moment my attention was drawn to an unexpected sight. At a distance of five hundred paces, at the turn of a high **promontory**, appeared a high, tufted, dense forest. It was composed of trees of moderate height, formed like umbrellas, with exact geometrical outlines. The currents of wind seemed to have had no effect upon their shape, and in the midst of the windy blasts they stood unmoved and firm, just like a clump of **petrified** cedars.

[4] I hastened forward. I could not give any name to these singular creations. Were they some of the two hundred thousand species of vegetables known hitherto, and did they claim a place of their own in the **lacustrine flora**? No; when we arrived under their shade my surprise turned into admiration. There stood before me **productions** of earth, but of gigantic stature, which my uncle immediately named.

[5] "It is only a forest of mushrooms," said he.

Jules Verne

> **prodigious** *adj.* remarkably or impressively great
> **titanic** *adj.* extremely powerful, strong, important or large; like a Titan (a giant god in ancient Greek mythology)
> **pellucid** *adj.* transparently clear (pronounced pe/loo/sid)
> **promontory** *n.* high ground that juts out into water
> **petrified** *adj.* turned to stone; terrified
> **lacustrine flora** *n.* list of plants that grow by lakes
> **productions** – old fashioned word for products

Session 5 Going back and looking into the future

1 **a** Scan the extract for the words *singular* and *hitherto*. Work out what they mean from the context.
   b Choose a modern word to use in their place.
   c Use each word in a sentence of your own.
2 **a** Scan the extract for the word *titanic*. What class of word is it?
   b *The Titanic was an enormous cruise liner that sank in 1912 after colliding with an iceberg.* What class of word is *Titanic* in this sentence?
   c Why do you think the ship was given its name?
3 *Petra* means 'rock' in Latin. Explain *petrified* in the context of the extract.

6 Working with voices and moods

A Use the active voice and the passive voice.

1 Are these sentences active or passive? How can you tell?

> **Language focus**
>
> The **active voice** is when the subject does the action to someone or something:
>
> Giovanni rode the bike.
>
> subject + active verb + direct object
>
> The **passive voice** is when the subject has the action done to it
>
> The bike was ridden by Giovanni.
>
> subject + passive verb + preposition + agent
>
> Passive verbs have a 'helping' verb (*to be*) + past participle: The bag <u>was dropped</u>. The clothes <u>are damaged</u>.
>
> The helping verb agrees with the subject and indicates the tense.

Example: *Jehan made the sandwiches.* → Active – Jehan is doing the action.
   a The gate was opened by the girl.
   b The apple was given to the teacher by the class.
   c Lorcan climbed the tree in two minutes.
2 Rewrite each of the sentences above in the opposite voice: change passive to active, or active to passive.

3 Put these sentences into the passive voice.

Example: Khalid won the race. → The race was won by Khalid.

   a The porter carried the bag.
   b Babalwa picked the flowers.
   c The monkeys hid the nuts in the tree.

B The passive voice can be used to leave out unimportant details. It can also build suspense by hiding the person who does the action.

1 Discuss the reasons for using the passive voice in these sentences.
   a The door was slowly pushed open …
   b Lunch will be provided at the event.
   c A parcel had been left on the table – with no note.

2 Write two passive voice sentences for each reason you identified.

3 *My attention was drawn to an unexpected sight.* Suggest why Jules Verne used the passive voice in this sentence.

C Regular past participles end in **ed**.

1 a Write the past participle of these verbs.

> laugh cry smile slam obey

   b Tell each other the rule you followed each time.
   c Think of another example for each rule.

2 a Write the past participle of these verbs.

> fly grow sing run think bring

Tip

The past participle is often the same as the simple past form.

   b List three other irregular verbs in your learning journal.

D Talking about the past and the future often involves *If* clauses.

Language focus

If clauses (also called conditionals) say what will or might happen in the present or future, or what could have happened, but didn't happen, in the past. The main clause is always the result of the *If* clause.

> If I take a torch, I will need batteries.
>
>   *If* clause   main clause

Session 6 Working with voices and moods

1. Some conditionals could happen but others are impossible. How likely are these conditionals?

   Example: *If you had studied, you would have passed.* → *Impossible, because it has already happened.*

   a If a spaceship gets too hot, it melts.
   b If the bus is late, she will miss the rocket launch.
   c If I went back in time, I would like to meet Queen Cleopatra.

2. Complete these conditional sentences to build suspense.

   a If only Saud had …
   b If she had not looked up at that moment, Martha …
   c Astrid thought, "I wonder what will happen if I …"

3. Invent your own conditional sentences to build suspense.

> **Tip**
> If the *If* clause comes first, separate it from the main clause with a comma.

7 Working with chapters, paragraphs and connectives

A Paragraphs are important – just imagine if everything we read was always in one long paragraph.

- Hmm … paragraph …?
- What is it? A sentence or group of sentences on the same theme or idea.
- Why start a new one? A new idea, a change in direction or scene (e.g. a new person talking).
- How long should it be? Any length!

1. Discuss the main idea or topic in each paragraph of the extract from *A Journey to the Interior of the Earth* on page 67. Why was each new paragraph started?

> **Tip**
> Chapter titles give clues about the theme or events in the chapter.

Unit 4 Time passing

2   In groups, choose a chapter each from your reading book and discuss it.
    a   Does your chapter have a title?
    b   What is the chapter's main theme or episode?
    c   How does it link to the chapters before and after?
3   Focus on three or four of the paragraphs.
    a   How long are the paragraphs? Short? Long? A variety?
    b   What is the main idea in each?
    c   Why was each new paragraph started?

B Different connectives do different jobs.

1   Create a mind map to organise these connectives according to their purpose.

> next   later   before   then   although   finally   unlike
> like   as well as   compared with   in addition to   however
> because   and   but   as a result   therefore   otherwise

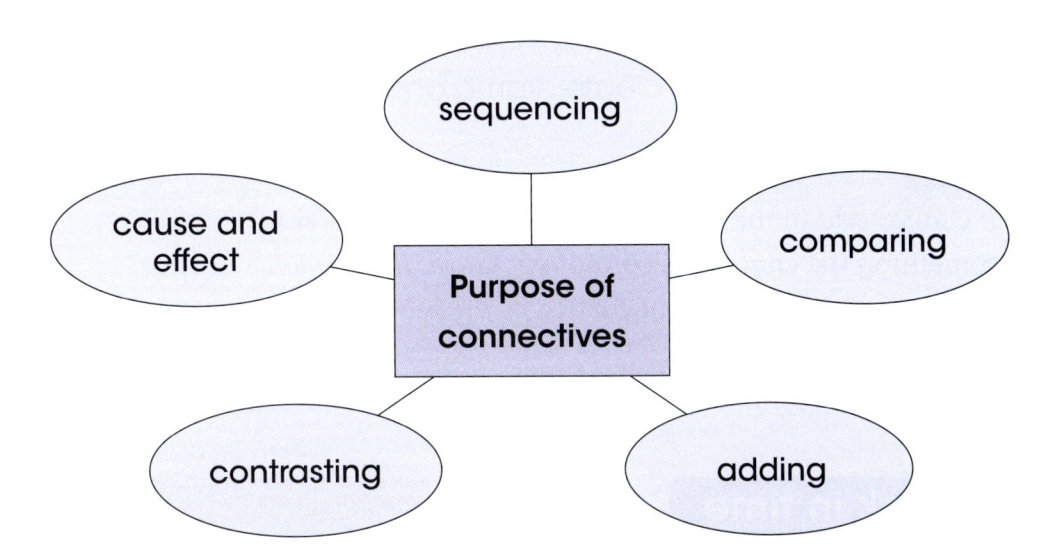

Purpose of connectives:
- sequencing
- comparing
- adding
- contrasting
- cause and effect

2   Which connectives in the extract on page 67 are used to:
    a   link clauses and sentences within paragraphs?
    b   link paragraphs to each other?
3   Are the answers to the previous question surprising? Why?

8 Write paragraphs describing fictional surroundings

A ✎ Descriptive paragraphs need imagination, detail and carefully chosen words. Axel and the professor encounter a dramatic waterfall and a forest of mushrooms. What will you encounter in your story?

1. Plan some details for Chapter 2 of your *Readaloudathon* science fiction story, using the planning table you started in Session 4. Think of ideas and words to describe the imaginary surroundings and jot them down.

2. Write a first draft of Chapter 2. Include:
   - a description of the setting and scenery
   - the build-up to what the characters see
   - details of what they see
   - their reaction and clues on how it will affect their new lives
   - connectives to make links within and between paragraphs.

3. Review your paragraphs carefully and work on your word choice and sentence construction to create drama and suspense.

> *What will your characters see? Something dramatic, creepy, comic, bizarre? Unusual scenes need unusual words!*

Tip
If clauses add to the suspense, especially if they refer to something the characters cannot yet know. *If Yolandah had noticed the flash of light emitted by the pebble …*

4. Read your paragraphs to a talk partner and ask for feedback.

9 Going back in time

A 👥 Time travel is another popular science fiction theme.
- If you had a time machine, when would you visit? Prepare a short speech to explain to others when and where you would go, who you would like to meet and why.

Chitty Chitty Bang Bang Flies Again

¹As Mum reached for the phone, Chitty lurched into reverse. Mum was thrown back into her seat. The phone tumbled to the floor. Suddenly the big shiny handle of Chitty's Chronojuster clunked to the bottom of its slot. Before they knew it, the car was speeding backwards down the middle lane.

²"Dad! You can't do this!" yelled Jem. "You're driving backwards down the motorway …"

³Lucy couldn't bear to look. Little Harry put his fingers in his ears. Jem stared in horrified fascination at the cars behind them rushing towards them. Except they weren't rushing towards them. They seemed to be going backwards too. It wasn't a motorway any more, just an ordinary road.

⁴"That's good," said Dad. "Trees are good."

⁵But he couldn't help but notice that the lane no longer had tarmac and road signs. It was just a track, a white dusty track cut into the chalk. The trees too were surprisingly tall. They were thicker. The air was damp and hot. The undergrowth was thick and steamy. So thick and steamy that Chitty had to stop to catch her breath (the engine was air-cooled).

⁶"Dinosaurs!" shouted Little Harry.

⁷"Yes, yes, when we get home we'll find your dinosaur," said Mum. "Now shush while I check the map. We seem to be lost."

⁸But Jem knew that you should never tell Little Harry to be quiet. Never ignore what he was saying. If Little Harry said dinosaurs, then that strange, heavy thumping that seemed to be coming nearer and nearer through the trees … that splintering of wood and crunching of rocks … that hideous, **mucousy** roar that almost deafened you …

⁹"I know this sounds strange," said Mum, pointing nervously off to the left, "but isn't that …?"

¹⁰"Dinosaurs!" yelled Little Harry.

¹¹"Tyrannosaurus rex, to be precise," said Lucy, "from the Latin for 'king of the terrible lizards'."

¹²"The word today," said Dad, "would seem to be **Jurassic**."

¹³"Not to be picky," observed Lucy as the giant beast came crashing towards them through the trees, "but I think you'll find that the word today is actually **Cretaceous**."

¹⁴"Dinosaurs!"

¹⁵"I think Chitty just engaged her Chronojuster," said Jem, leafing quickly through the logbook and manual. "It says here, 'Do not engage the Chronojuster unless –'" he looked up – "'time travel is required …'"

Frank Cottrell Boyce

mucousy *adj.* to do with mucus (thick liquid in the throat or nose)
Jurassic *adj.* period from 205 million to 144 million years ago
Cretaceous *adj.* period following the Jurassic era

B 🕮 💬 👤 Ian Fleming wrote a story about Chitty Chitty Bang Bang, a car with many talents, in the 1960s. Nearly 50 years later, Frank Cottrell Boyce wrote a series of sequels about Chitty's adventures in the 21st century.

1. In groups, read the extract on page 73 from Frank Cottrell Boyce's story *Chitty Chitty Bang Bang Flies Again*. Skim over the extract first to get the general idea, then re-read it in more detail, taking the parts of the narrator, Dad, Mum, Jem, Lucy and Harry.
2. Take turns to summarise the events in your own words.
3. How did each of the children react to what was happening?
4. Perform your reading. Sit as if you are in Chitty. Stay in character using movement and expression even when you are not speaking.

C 📝 At the start of this story, Chitty is an old camper van. By the end she has all her original fixtures and fittings back and a few more!

1. List the features that make this a science fiction story.
2. This extract is the ending of the book. How has the author tried to make the reader want to read the next book in the series?

10 Spelling, punctuation and structure challenge

A 🕮 💬 AZ Test your knowledge and understanding!

1. Find evidence to complete the following paragraph about the story.

> I think the Chitty extract is a modern/classic text because ... Some examples are ... In addition ... Finally...

2. What is the purpose of the brackets in paragraph 5?
3. Why does the author use the ellipsis four times in paragraphs 8 and 9?
4. a What sort of word is *Chronojuster*? Would it be in the dictionary?
   b *Chrono* means 'time' in ancient Greek. How does this help you decide what a Chronojuster does?
   c What other word has it been created from?

5 Find and explain two different uses of the apostrophe.

6 Explain the punctuation in the final sentence of the extract.

7 Use examples from the narrative and dialogue to answer these questions.

   a What narrative person is used?

   b What are the main tenses used? Give reasons.

   c Would you describe the writing style as formal or informal?

8 a What is the reason for the very short paragraphs?

   b The author uses strings of short sentences. What effect is does this create?

B AZ Focus on spelling rules and strategies.

1 Look at these words. Identify four word endings of at least four letters that all sound the same.

> spoon   electrician   lemon   possession   portion
> fortune   mansion   captain   percussion
> divine   fiction   magician   confusion

2 The suffix **cian** means 'one who has specific skills'. How many words do you know with this suffix? What do they all describe?

3 a Which of these words is the odd one out in terms of its sound?

> television   occasion   division   persuasion
> revision   mansion   supervision   decision

   b What root word appears in several of the words?

   c How can this help you with spelling?

   d Think of as many words as you can ending in **tion** and **sion**. Can you devise rules to help you remember their spelling?

Tip

tion is the most common 'shun' sound suffix.

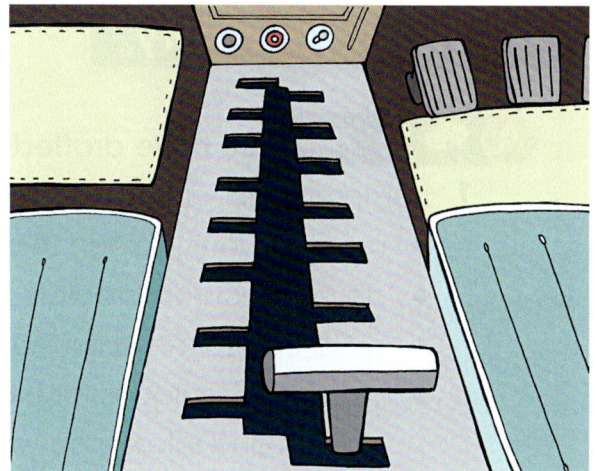

Session 10 Spelling, punctuation and structure challenge

11 Finish your story

A 💬 📝 🔤 You have drafted Chapters 1 and 2; now finish your story.

1 Remember to:
   - mention your 'golden thread' object in every chapter
   - develop your characters
   - build up suspense for the climax
   - include techniques for dramatic effect like brackets for asides, *If* clauses, ellipses and interesting word choices
   - stick to the story structure you planned.
2 Get feedback from a talk partner and act on any suggestions.
3 Proofread and underline any spelling, grammar or punctuation errors. Make corrections.
4 Present your final version in neat handwriting or using ICT. Double-check your spelling using a spellcheck tool or dictionary.

12 Take part in a *Readaloudathon!*

A 📖 💬 👥 Celebrate your stories in a class *Readaloudathon*.

1 In groups of five or six, take turns to tell your stories. Bring the story to life using expression, movement, pace, volume and dramatic pauses.
2 Did you guess the 'golden thread' in each story early on or later? (See Activity B on page 60)
3 Send a spokesperson to another group to summarise the stories and say whether the group identified all the 'golden thread' objects.

Readaloudathon!

5 Poles apart

The expression 'There are two sides to a coin' reminds us that there are always different views about a topic. In this unit you'll read and summarise information, make comparisons and discuss controversial issues. You'll argue a case from one point of view, give a balanced report showing both sides of an argument, and express your opinions in a debate.

Vocabulary to learn and use: Arctic, Antarctic, continent, argument, balanced, biased, opposing, emotive

1 Describe and compare

A These places may not look poles apart, but they are!

1 What do you think the expression 'poles apart' means? Where do you think it comes from?
2 Do you live in a hot or a cold place? What is it like? Do you prefer hot or cold places?
3 Describe what you see in the pictures. Compare them.

Session 1 Describe and compare

4 With a partner, read these facts and decide which describe the Arctic and which describe the Antarctic.

a One is a continent while the other is an ocean.

b Both are desert regions although one is considered the largest desert on Earth.

c One has a permanent population but the other doesn't.

d Both are cold however, one is colder.

e One has penguins whereas the other has polar bears.

5 Compare answers with the rest of the class and agree on a final conclusion.

> **Did you know?**
> A desert is an area that has very little rain and not much plant or animal life. Areas of sand, rock or ice can be deserts.

B Adjectives of comparison are used to compare two or more things, such as *Antarctica is the highest, driest, windiest, emptiest, coldest place on Earth.*

1 Draw a table in your notebook and complete the adjectives of comparison.

Adjective	Comparative adjective	Superlative adjective
high	higher	highest
		driest
		windiest
		emptiest

2 Use a thesaurus to find more superlative adjectives to describe Antarctica.

Unit 5 Poles apart

C 📝 Connectives are useful in sentences that compare things, for example ***Both places are cold yet one place is much colder.***

1 Write sentences comparing the Arctic and the Antarctic using connectives. You can refer to the sentences in A to give you some ideas.

> but   although   yet   since   however
> while   on the other hand   whereas

2 Some connectives work in pairs. Complete each sentence with a pair of connectives.

> both/and   whether/or   not only/but also   neither/nor   either/or

   a They can't decide … to travel north … south.
   b I enjoy … cold places … hot places.
   c I am … keen … excited about living in Antarctica.

2 Summarise and write paragraphs

Antarctica

- Antarctica is the southernmost and fifth-largest continent on Earth.
- 98% of Antarctica is covered by ice up to 1.6 km thick (1 mile).
- The coldest recorded temperature on Earth occurred in 1983 at Vostok Station, Antarctica, measuring −89.2 °C (−128.6 °F).
- Humans do not live in Antarctica permanently, but several thousand people live and work at research stations temporarily.
- Only a few animals, such as penguins and seals, live in Antarctica.
- Antarctica contains around 90% of the ice on Earth.

The Arctic

- The Arctic region is the northernmost part of Earth and contains the geographic North Pole.
- Indigenous people live in the Arctic.
- Small shrubs, herbs and mosses can grow in warmer parts of the Arctic.
- Animals of the Arctic include polar bears, wolverines, squirrels, birds, walrus and seals.
- The Arctic has valuable natural resources including fish, oil, gas and various minerals.

A Make notes about the polar regions.

1 Read the information about Antarctica and the Arctic.
2 Write two headings in your notebook and list key words from the facts.

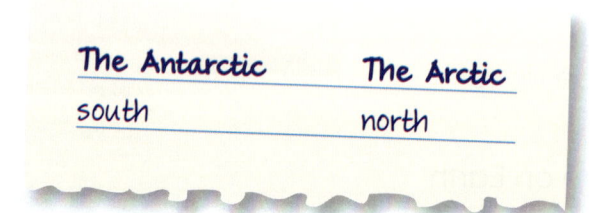

The Antarctic	The Arctic
south	north

B Work out the meanings of words.

1 The prefix **anti** comes from a Greek word meaning 'opposite'.
   a What do you think the name Antarctic means?
   b Make the opposites of these words by adding the prefix **anti**.

   clockwise   cyclone   freeze

2 Find other prefixes that change word meanings to the opposite.
3 What does the prefix **ante** mean? Find words with this prefix.

Unit 5 Poles apart

Did you know?

The word *Arctic* comes from the Greek word *arktos* meaning 'bear'. The Arctic is so called because it is below the northern **constellation** of the Great Bear.

constellation *n.* a group of stars in the sky that seem from Earth to form a pattern and have been given a name

C Describe the polar regions to someone who is trying to decide which region to visit. Write two short paragraphs of a non-chronological report describing what each place has to offer.

Tip

In a non-chronological report, the sequence of information is not always important.

1. Use your key words from Activity A to write two paragraphs.
   - Write a heading to describe the topic.
   - Introduce each paragraph with a topic sentence.
   - Use your own words to describe each place.
   - Use no more than 50 words in each paragraph.
2. Choose an appropriate connective from page 71 to begin the second paragraph so that the paragraphs flow together e.g. *On the other hand … .*

Language focus

A paragraph consists of a number of sentences that deal with one idea or topic. A paragraph consists of a topic sentence and supporting detail. A topic sentence introduces the main idea of the paragraph. Connectives link ideas and help paragraphs flow together.

Session 2 Summarise and write paragraphs

3 Analyse a news report

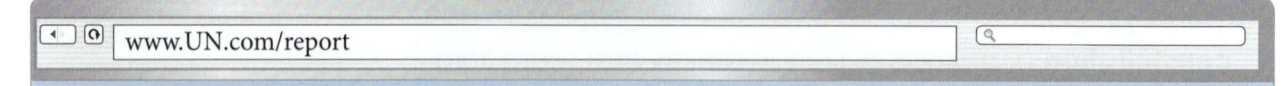

A Read and understand a news report.

www.UN.com/report

Home | Reports | Reviews | New releases | Best of 2013

Human activity responsible for global warming: UN report

A group of scientists associated with the United Nations has just issued a report on 'climate change'.

The Intergovernmental Panel on Climate Change has confirmed that human habits and activity are responsible for global warming and for higher sea levels. If this continues, according to the report, there will be more serious heat waves, more melting of land ice, and dramatic changes in plant and animal life. Because it is a draft, the report is still being reviewed, but experts in climate change believe there won't be many changes in the final version.

The report is published by a different group of scientists every five or six years, and is considered the standard on the risks of climate change. Each report has found more evidence that the planet is warming and that humans are the cause. Some critics believe that the current situation is more likely due to short-term factors or weather cycles. They believe that the climate situation will change on its own eventually. But the UN report says the reality is clear and the facts are there.

Luckily, because humans cause the problem, humans can help solve the problem. Everyone can use less energy (light and electricity), recycle and reuse, and use their cars less. If this happens, less carbon dioxide will be released into the air and the air closest to the Earth will cool down. And that would be a good thing.

Nancy Miller

McCarty Glacier, Kenai Fjords National Park, Alaska, photographed in 1909.

McCarty Glacier, Kenai Fjords National Park, Alaska, photographed in 2004.

1 What is the report about? Skim the headline and lead to find out.
2 Identify key characteristics of a report.

> **Tip**
>
> Look at the language and layout. Does it have paragraphs, diagrams and headings?

Any volunteers? How can you tell that this is a type of news report?

3 Read the report in detail. Discuss unfamiliar words and try to work out their meanings from the context before checking in a dictionary.
4 Does the report contain mainly facts or mainly opinions?

> **Tip**
>
> A fact is something that actually happened or can be proved. An opinion is what someone thinks or believes, and is often expressed with words like *They think …; It is considered …; She believes …; In his view …*

5 Find some opinions in the text.
6 The report is described as a *draft* report. What does this mean?

B Focus on the purpose and language of the report.

1 Who is the news report for? What is its purpose?
2 Choose words that describe the style of this report:

> friendly   funny   formal   personal   impersonal

3 *Luckily, because humans cause the problem, humans can help solve the problem.* Replace one word in this statement so that it means the same but sounds more formal.
4 Explain the purpose of the following punctuation in the report:
   a the colon in the headline
   b the speech marks in the first sentence
   c the comma in long sentences in the second paragraph.
5 Has the reporter used Standard English to write this report? How can you tell?

Session 3 Analyse a news report

C **Identify and summarise the main idea.**

1 Make notes of the details in the report. Write key words only.

> **Tip**
>
> Use the inverted pyramid to help you summarise the text. (See page 32.)

2 Summarise the news report in no more than 50 words. Begin with a lead sentence and use your own words.

4 Have a discussion

A **In pairs, read and discuss an explanation of climate change.**

| Carbon dioxide (CO_2) is part of the atmosphere. Some CO_2 is created naturally but some comes from fumes of cars, aeroplanes and the generation of electricity. | As CO_2 collects in the atmosphere it acts like a blanket over the Earth; heat cannot escape and so the Earth heats up. | Excess heat is absorbed by the ocean and distributed. This helps regulate the temperature. | The extra heat causes the water temperature to rise. The warmer waters melt ice in the Polar regions, raising sea levels. |

1 Explain climate change to a talk partner in your own words. Remember that the sequence is important here.
2 What role do humans play in this process?
3 Some argue that climate change is a natural process and would happen anyway. What do you think?
4 What could humans do to help slow the process down?
5 What could you do to make a difference?

B **With your talk partner, decide if you agree or disagree with the statements at the top of page 85.**

1 Copy these sentences into your notebook. After each sentence, add two statements of your own, one agreeing and one disagreeing.

2 Share your statements with another group. Compare your views.

> Climate change is a natural process and there is nothing humans can do to stop it.

I agree because …
I disagree because …

> Humans should be more responsible and use less electricity.

I agree because …
I disagree because …

Use conditional clauses to express possibility.

Language focus

Conditional clauses express the possibility of something that may happen in the future.

If the rain stops, we can play outside.
We can play outside if the rain stops.

Notice that the subordinate clause (or *If* clause) can go before or after the main clause.

If the subordinate clause goes before the main clause, you can add a comma to create a pause and help the sense.

1 Complete these sentences with a main clause.
   a If everyone became more aware, …
   b If the ice in the polar regions melts, …
   c If we want to reduce car fumes, …
   d If there is too much air pollution, …
   e If all the plankton in the sea dies, …

2 Rewrite your sentences, putting the subordinate clause after the main clause.

Tip

A main clause is the main idea of a sentence. It must have a subject and a finite verb to make sense and stand alone.

How did I do?

- Did I make notes and summarise information into a short report?
- Did I analyse a news report and identify its key characteristics?
- Could I confidently express my views on a controversial issue?
- Did I write good sentences with conditional clauses?

5 Keep it formal

A How formal a text is depends on its audience and purpose.

> ### Language focus
>
> A report uses Standard English, which means the language is correct and formal. When writing a report, you should:
> - avoid colloquial expressions and contractions
> - avoid a personal style that uses *I* or *we* – write in the third person instead:
>   *We feel concerned about the environment.* (personal style)
>   *Many people feel concerned about the environment.* (impersonal style)

1. Why are pronouns so useful when we write? What effect do they have on a text?
2. Identify the first, second and third person pronouns:

   > I   you   he/him   she/her   it   we/us   they/them

3. Rewrite these sentences in your notebook, replacing the first person pronouns with the word in brackets to make them sound impersonal.
   a. If climate change continues, our planet will be in trouble. (*the*)
   b. Our report reveals important evidence. (*this*)
   c. My draft is due to be reviewed. (*the*)
   d. We are finding evidence to support climate change. (*scientists*)
   e. If we rode bikes, there would be less air pollution. (*everyone*)
4. Rewrite these sentences without using contractions.
   a. It's become a problem that they'll have to solve.
   b. If you're concerned about what's happening, you'll need to get involved.
   c. It'll take time to improve the situation but that's to be expected.

6 The passive voice

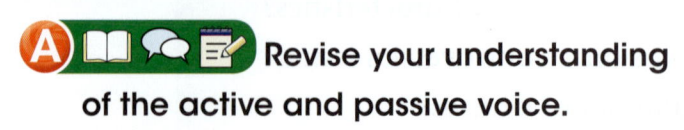

A Revise your understanding of the active and passive voice.

Language focus

In the active voice, the subject does the action: Scientists have issued a report.
In the passive voice the person or thing doing the action (the agent) is no longer the subject: A report has been issued by scientists.
To find the agent, ask: *who or what is doing the action?*
Sometimes the agent is hidden or it is not necessary to know. For example:

   A report was issued.

Ask: *who issued a report?* There are various possible answers.
The passive voice is useful for making general statements, especially if you want to imply something or leave open various options.

1. Look at the **Language focus** box, then explain to your talk partner why you would use the passive voice in a formal report.

2. Copy the following sentences in your notebook. Underline the action and circle the agent (the doer of the action). If the agent is hidden, write *hidden*.

   Example: The problem <u>will be solved</u> by (everyone).

   a The draft report will be reviewed by the committee.
   b Less electricity should be used.
   c The situation can be improved.
   d Recommendations have been made by scientists.
   e Responsibility must be taken.

B If the agent is hidden, it implies that there are various options to the outcome of the statement.

1. Compare these sentences. Which one is the most general statement?
   - The situation can be improved.
   - The situation can be improved by interested scientists.
   - The situation can be improved by anyone who would like to get involved.

2. Complete this sentence in three or four different ways, giving a different agent each time.

   Less electricity can be used.

   Example: Less electricity can be used by schoolchildren.

3. Add some examples of sentences in the passive voice to your learning journal.

Session 6 Using the passive voice

7 Read and assess a balanced report

A A balanced report presents all aspects of an issue, then leaves the readers to make up their own minds.

Is it time to ban cars from city centres?

Introduction – state the issue

Air pollution is a serious issue and it affects us all directly. Action may be needed to reduce air pollution created by the traffic on our roads.

Points for

In the past few decades a significant increase in the number of cars on the road has resulted in more carbon dioxide emissions. *(Topic sentence)* Scientists are warning that high levels of CO_2 in the atmosphere cause the earth to heat up. As a result, we are experiencing more extreme weather patterns. In addition, air pollution in cities causes health problems like asthma. A ban on cars in city centres would therefore reduce air pollution and also improve traffic jams and health issues.

Points against

On the other hand, such a ban could create other problems. *(Topic sentence)* In some cities, public transport is expensive, unreliable or non-existent. In addition, public transport systems would need to be upgraded to cope with greater demand; this requires time and money. Furthermore, personal choice is an issue. *(Use of connectives)* For example some people enjoy using public transport but others feel safer in their cars than on a bus or a train. Hence, they may object to being forced to use another mode of transport.

Conclusion – offer a recommendation

While there is clearly an urgent need to reduce air pollution, we could achieve this in a number of ways. Rather than banning cars in cities, people could be made aware of the issues and encouraged to use less fuel and make use of public transport where possible.

Unit 5 Poles apart

Features of a balanced report

✓ It has a heading and is divided into paragraphs.

✓ The introduction states the issue.

✓ The conclusion summarises both points giving recommendations.

✓ It is fair to both sides.

✓ Each view is supported with reasons or evidence.

✓ The language is formal and **unbiased**.

✓ Paragraphs link and flow together

unbiased *adj.* able to judge fairly because you are not influenced by your own opinions

1. Read the report on page 88 about traffic in cities. Notice the key characteristics.
2. Is the report balanced? Assess it by checking for the features in the list.
3. Write your own guidelines on how to write a balanced report. Include any other features you think are important.

8 Language techniques

A When you present two sides of an argument, you can use connectives to combine or connect your points for greater effect or clarity.

> however   therefore   for example   despite   although
> in addition   firstly   since   as a result
> on the other hand   linked to this   similarly   as well as

1. Scan the report in the previous session to locate the connectives.
   Find examples of connectives that are used to:
   - **a** link two opposing views
   - **b** link two similar views
   - **c** support a view by giving an example
   - **d** add weight to the point being made.

2 Rewrite these sentences in your notebook, adding a connective from the connective box for clarity.
   a Some believe cars are essential … others say they are a luxury.
   b Homework is here to stay … it is not very popular.
   c Pocket money gives young people freedom … independence.
   d Electricity is useful … we should use it sparingly.
   e Air pollution is caused by cars … factory fumes.

B Reports are written in a particular tense, according to their purpose. News reports describe events in the past tense, but non-chronological reports and balanced reports may be in the present tense. A report may also use the future tense to predict something that might happen.

1 What tense is used in the opening statement of the report about traffic in cities?
2 Can you identify any sentences in the past tense? Explain why.
3 Identify examples of conditional verbs that express the possibility of something happening in the future.

> **Tip**
>
> Conditional verbs include the words *could*, *would*, *may* or *might*.

4 Rewrite these sentences in the future tense by using an appropriate conditional verb.

Example: Air pollution has become a problem → Air pollution could become a problem.

   a A change in weather patterns will occur.
   b People can be more responsible.
   c Air pollution will cause health issues.
   d Animal habitats can be affected.
   e The Earth will heat up.

How did I do?

- Did I practise using formal language?
- Do I understand the passive voice and how to use it in a report?
- Did I analyse the language in a balanced report?

9 Write a balanced report

A Write your own balanced report on a controversial issue.

1. Choose a topic and note your ideas for and against it.
   - Can children help to reduce climate change?
   - Should the school plan a compulsory trip to Antarctica?
   - Are wild, endangered animals better off in zoos?
2. Plan your report. Use the set of guidelines you wrote in Session 7.
3. Remember to use the language techniques you've learned about.
4. Proofread and edit your work. Ask a talk partner to read your report and see if it feels like you're taking a side. If so, change those parts that sound biased.
5. Present your final version using neat, joined-up handwriting or ICT.
6. Send it to someone in charge or have it published for others to read.

Introduction
Conclusion
Be fair to both sides of the argument
Use formal language
Third person pronouns
No contractions
Use passive voice to make general statements
Use connectives to link ideas

Tip

Think about who will read your report. You could put it in your school newsletter or send it to an environmental website, magazine or news agency!

10 A biased view

A The opposite of a balanced view is a biased view, giving only one side of an issue according to the writer's personal opinion. Biased language can be **emotive** as the writer tries to sway the reader's opinion.

emotive *adj.* full of emotion

Any volunteers?
When is it appropriate to be biased?

The shrinking world of penguins

The tuxedoed seabirds' homeland is melting beneath their feet as global warming strikes hard in Antarctica and elsewhere.

As Dee Boersma sees it, penguins could be environmentalists' best allies in the fight against global warming.

"Mounting evidence points to climate change as the greatest threat to penguins, especially those species breeding in the Antarctic region," she says.

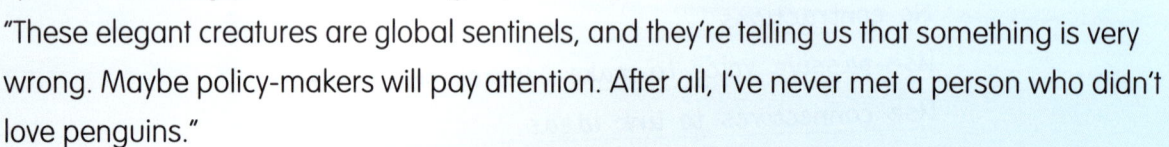

"These elegant creatures are global sentinels, and they're telling us that something is very wrong. Maybe policy-makers will pay attention. After all, I've never met a person who didn't love penguins."

Penguins cope with a host of problems, from habitat loss, alien animals, guano mining, deadly trawl nets and capricious weather systems to food shortages from overfishing.

1 Look at the photo and title of this article. What do they suggest?
2 Is this a literal or figurative image of what is happening to penguins? Explain why.
3 What effect does it have on the reader?
4 Find examples of figurative language in the rest of the text. What is the writer suggesting in each one?
5 Write a more balanced title for this article.

Unit 5 Poles apart

B **Vocabulary can be used to sound more or less emotive.**

1 Identify the emotive words in these sentences.

   Example: Penguins <u>are falling prey</u> to climate change.

   a These elegant creatures are global sentinels.
   b Penguins in Antarctica are a dying breed.
   c Penguins cope with a host of problems.
   d Everyone must take responsibility for this crisis.
   e I've never met a person who didn't love penguins.

2 Rewrite the sentences in question 1 using less emotive vocabulary.

   Example: Penguins are being affected by climate change.

C **Proverbs are old sayings used to express a general truth.**

- Choose a proverb and use it in a sentence about the environment.

> Live and let live.
> A guilty conscience needs no accuser.
> Every cloud has a silver lining.
> What goes around comes around.
> None so blind as those who will not see.
> Waste not, want not.

11 Argue a case

A Write a **biased** paragraph of about 10 lines, arguing that people's actions have consequences on the habitat of animals.

1 Write an emotive heading and a strong opening statement.
2 Support this view with two or three clear points, linked by connectives:

> Furthermore   In addition   Consequently   Clearly   As a result

3 Conclude by stating what you feel should be done.
4 Read out your paragraph in groups. Whose sounded the most convincing?

12 Have a class debate

A 📖 💬 A debate is where each person gets to present their side of an argument, either individually or as a team.

Latest evidence: Human activity not responsible for climate change

New report dismisses human-caused global warming

Scientists agree – climate change is inevitable!

Arctic melt – not our fault!

1 What is the main idea presented in these headlines?
2 How does it differ from other views on this topic?
3 Are you surprised to realise that there are two sides to this issue?

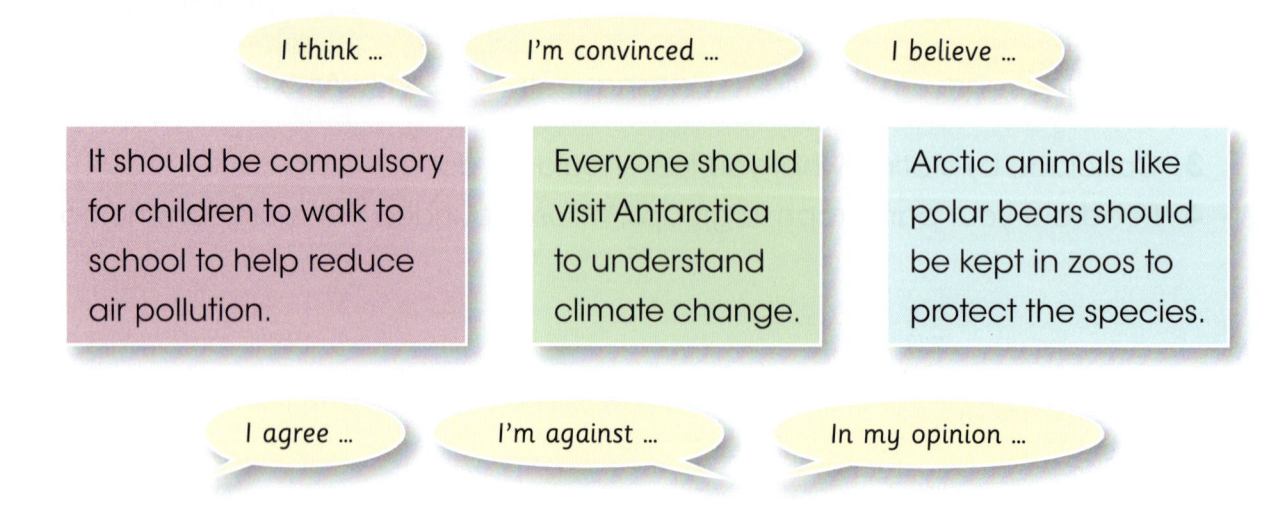

B 💬 📝 👥 It's time to take sides! Work in small groups and have a debate.

I think …   *I'm convinced …*   *I believe …*

| It should be compulsory for children to walk to school to help reduce air pollution. | Everyone should visit Antarctica to understand climate change. | Arctic animals like polar bears should be kept in zoos to protect the species. |

I agree …   *I'm against …*   *In my opinion …*

94   Unit 5 Poles apart

1. Read the statements and agree or disagree with each one.
2. In a debate, opposing teams compete with one another. The aim is for each team to convince the audience of their argument and disprove the other team's argument.
   a. Choose one topic you would like to debate and make a list of points for and against your topic.
   b. Choose a side and note down your ideas for a good speech.
3. Write out your speech in full and practise saying it aloud.

> **Tip**
>
> In order to make your point clear, remember to use connectives such as *firstly, in addition, moreover, therefore* and *finally*.

Title
Introduction – state my position clearly
Make three convincing points in my argument (1, 2, 3)
Conclusion – summarise and try to convince the audience

4. Arrange the room ready for the debate.
5. Each team member has the chance to present his or her speech.
6. After the speeches the audience can ask the teams questions.
7. Finally the audience chooses the winner by voting on which team was more convincing.

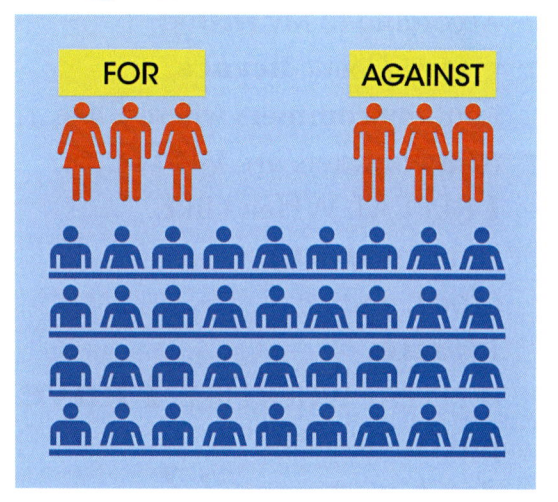

How did I do?

- Did I write a balanced report?
- Do I understand what a biased view is?
- Did I argue a case in writing and have a debate?

6 Words at play

Writing has so many rules but sometimes you can bend them to express yourself and be creative! In this unit you'll see how writers use poetic licence in creative ways to entertain and make a point. You'll experiment with words and grammar rules and have fun creating your own nonsense!

Vocabulary to learn and use: nonsense, poetic licence, visual, auditory, portmanteau word, metre

1 Poetic licence

According to my Mood

I have **poetic** licence, i Wri**T**e th**E** way i wa**N**t.
i *drop* my **full stops** where *i* like …
MY CAPITAL Lete**R**s go where i li**KE**,
i **order** from MY PEN, i verse **the way** i like
    (**i do** *my spelling write*)
According to My **mo**od.
i H**A**ve *p*oetic **licence**,
i put my **commers** where **i** like,,((()).
(((my brackets *are* **write**((
I REPEAT WHen i lik**E**.
i can't go ***rong***.
i ***look*** and i.c.
It's **rite**.
i**I** REPEAT WHen i lik**E**. **i have**
poetic licence!
don't question me?*?*?

Benjamin Zephaniah

A 📖 💬 **Poetry does not always obey the rules!**
  1 Skim over this poem. What do you notice?
  2 Take turns to read the poem aloud to a talk partner.

> **Tip**
> You can read it differently to your partner using your own expression!

3 Did you find it easy or difficult to read? Why?

4 How would you describe the poem?

- humorous
- personal
- informal
- unusual
- exaggerated
- rebellious

B 💬 📖 The voice in a poem may be the writer's own voice, or it may express the thoughts of someone else.

1 The title *According to my Mood* implies that the speaker is in a particular mood. What mood is it?

2 What do you think has caused the speaker to feel this way?

3 What view does the poem express? Do you agree with it?

4 Who is the poet?

5 Read a short biography to find out more about the poet and his views.

   a Who does he want to inspire with his poetry?

   b Does his style suit his audience?

   c What is his message?

   d What do you think about this?

Benjamin Zephaniah

Benjamin Obadiah Iqbal Zephaniah was born in 1958 in Britain. His writing is strongly influenced by the music and poetry of Jamaica. He began performing his poems at the age of ten! His mission is to make poetry come alive to children, teens and adults all over the world, including those who cannot read. He spends much of his time touring and performing in Asia, South America and Africa.

6 Now that you know a bit about the poet, do you think the voice in the poem is his own voice?

C **Poetic licence is often used in poetry for effect.**

1 What is poetic licence? Tell a talk partner.
2 Is the effect in the poem visual or **auditory** or both? To answer, think about how the punctuation guides the expression we read with, and how spelling affects pronunciation. Use examples of punctuation, capitalisation and spelling.

> **auditory** *adj.* to do with hearing

3 Where else is poetic licence used?
4 Write the poem out using correct grammar and spelling rules.
5 What difference does it make? Does the meaning or message change?

2 Compare poems

A **Compare two poems with similar themes.**

1 Read the poem on page 99 a few times on your own. Do you like it? Is it fun? Do you understand it?
2 In groups, discuss any words or phrases that need explaining.
3 Find the message in the poem and explain it in your own words.
4 What are the similarities and differences between *According to my Mood* and *poem: a reminder*?

> This poem gives some useful advice, if you can find it!

- message
- style
- subject
- tone
- **similarities**
- **differences**
- poetic licence
- narrative
- stanza structure
- rhyme scheme

Unit 6 Words at play

poem: a reminder

capitallett

    -ers prompting ev

        -ery line lines printed down the
        cen
        -tre of each page clear

       spaces between

       groups of these combine in a con

v
 e
  n
   t
    i
     o
      n

       of respectable age to mean read
care
       -fully each word we chose has

        rhythm and
        sound and
        sense this is

notprose

Robert Graves

---

in a convention of respectable age as people have agreed for some time
prose *n.* the ordinary language used in speaking/writing

5 **Enjambment** is when a phrase, clause or sentence in a line of poetry spills over into the next line. Find examples of enjambment in both poems.
6 Which poem would you prefer to read aloud? Why?

B Understand the context of the poem and who wrote it.

Robert Graves

Robert Graves (1895–1985) was a British poet and novelist who wrote about nature, love and war. He preferred to use traditional poetic techniques rather than modern experimental styles.

1 How long ago do you think this poem might have been written?
2 Did Robert Graves write about serious or light-hearted topics?
3 What style of poetry did he prefer?
4 What do you think 'experimental writing' is?
5 In what ways do a writer's life experiences impact his or her writing?

How did I do?

- Did I compare two poems?
- Did I express preferences about poems?

3 Do sounds and letters always agree?

Sounds and letters

When in English class we speak,
Why is break not rhymed with freak?
Will you tell me why it's true
That we say sew, but also few?

When a poet writes a verse
Why is horse not rhymed with worse?
Beard sounds not the same as heard,
Lord sounds not the same as word.

Cow is cow, but low is low
Shoe is never rhymed with toe.
Think of nose and dose and lose
Think of goose, but then of choose.

Confuse not comb with tomb or bomb,
Doll with roll, or home with some.
We have blood and food and good.
Mould is not pronounced like could.

There's pay and say, but paid and said.
"I will read", but "I have read".
Why say done, but gone and lone –
Is there any reason known?

To summarise, it seems to me
Sounds and letters disagree.

Lord Cromer

A Reading can be challenging, even for the most experienced reader!
1 In small groups, read the poem aloud, taking one stanza each.
2 Is the writer expressing his own feelings? How can you tell?
3 Who is the poem addressing? How do you know?
4 Would you describe the tone as serious, humorous or both? Why?

B Consider the structure of the poem.
1 How many stanzas are there and with how many lines?
2 Identify the rhyming pattern.
3 List the pairs of rhyming words in your notebook. Underline the letters that form the rhyme. Are they always the same letters?
4 Does the poem use end rhymes, internal rhymes or both? What effect does this have?

C **AZ** This poem offers the perfect opportunity to revise spelling, pronunciation and word classes in a fun way.

1 Identify words in the poem:
   a which have a homophone
   b that are homographs
   c with silent letters
   d with the **ee** sound
   e with the long **o** sound (as in *bone*).
2 Find three examples of words where the vowel blends are the same but the sound is completely different.
3 Identify five singular nouns in stanza 3.
4 Identify two plural nouns in the final stanza.
5 Which verbs are in the past tense and which are in the present?

> **Tip**
>
> A **homophone** is a word that has a different spelling but the same pronunciation as another word, like *no* and *know*.
>
> **Homographs** are different words with the same spelling e.g. *seal*.

D Try your hand at writing! Work in pairs.

1 Add one or two stanzas of your own to the poem.
   • Suggest words that are challenging to spell or pronounce.
   • Pair up words that rhyme but have different spellings.
   • Make sure your tone and rhyme scheme match the original poem.
2 Team up with another pair. Check and edit your stanzas.
   Put them together and read them aloud to the class.

> **Tip**
>
> Don't forget to write neatly, especially as you'll be reading aloud!

When I write, it's write not <u>right</u>,
I must be, not bee and see not <u>sea</u>!
It is a puzzle why we say
Day must rhyme with <u>neigh and slay</u>.

Spy my light kite high in the sky!

4 Made-up words and nonsense

Eletelephony

Once there was an elephant,
Who tried to use the telephant –
No! No! I mean an elephone
Who tried to use the telephone –
(Dear me! I am not certain quite
That even now I've got it right.)

Howe'er it was, he got his trunk
Entangled in the telephunk;
The more he tried to get it free,
The louder buzzed the telephee –
(I fear I'd better drop the song
Of elephop and telephong!)

Laura E. Richards

Did you know?

Nonsense poems are poems that sound silly, absurd or strange. Words seem to make sense but they actually don't. The poet invents or changes words.

A Some poets like to write nonsense poems and make up words for fun! Read *Eletelephony* with a talk partner.
1 Can you understand the **gist** of the poem?
2 Are the made-up words nouns, verbs or adjectives?
3 Why do you think the poet used made-up words?
4 Read the poem aloud, replacing the made-up words with real words. What effect does it have?

gist *n.* the basic idea

B Explore portmanteau words.

Language focus

When parts of words are put together and their meanings are combined in the new word, this is called a **portmanteau word**. For example *smog*, meaning 'smoky fog', is a combination of *smoke* and *fog*.

1 Parts of which real words make up the word *telephant*?

2 What do these common portmanteau words mean? Which words do they come from?

- **a** ginormous
- **b** Bollywood
- **c** infomercial
- **d** bionic
- **e** intercom
- **f** biopic
- **g** email
- **h** brunch

> ### Did you know?
> *Portmanteau* comes from the French word *portemanteau* – a large suitcase that opens into two compartments! Can you see why it's used in the context of an invented word?

3 A portmanteau word is different from a contraction. Write contractions of the following. **Example:** I am – I'm

- **a** will not
- **b** they are
- **c** he is
- **d** are not
- **e** you will

> ### Tip
> Use an apostrophe to show where letters have been left out.

4 A portmanteau word is also different from a compound word. Make compound words from these words e.g. tooth + brush → toothbrush:

> spoon   shell   be   tooth   tea   sun   hind   flower   brush   sea

5 List more portmanteau words, contractions and compound words in your learning journal.

> ### How did I do?
> - Did I identify poetry features?
> - Could I identify and use portmanteau words, contractions and compound words?

5 Have fun with words

A 📖 💬 The shape or form of a poem can add to its meaning.

1. What do you notice about the direction of the words in this poem?
2. How does this add to the meaning and impact of the words?
3. Identify the rhyming pattern.
4. Explain the wordplay and technique used in the title.

B 📝 💬 Try writing words in a different direction from usual for impact.

1. Choose a topic and think of different words to describe it – how it sounds, moves and feels, and the effect it has. For example, what shape do these words make?

river   pasta   shoelace   whirlpool   snake   road   worm   whirlwind

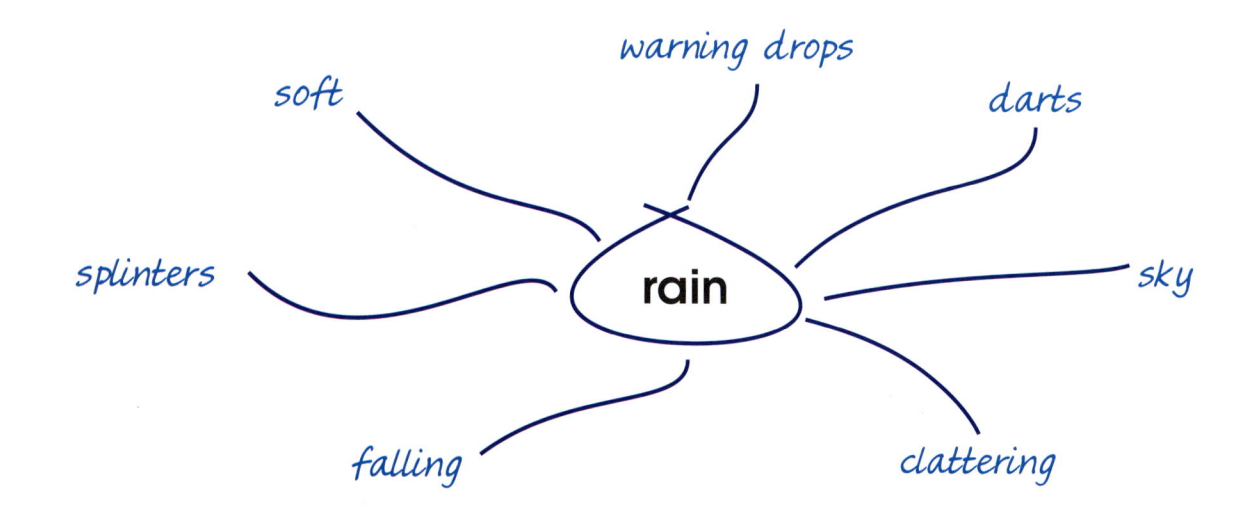

Amaized

Corn	all.	I	days.
grows	at	wind	for
in	here	my	daze
rows	I'm	way	a
so	know	through	in
green	will	maze	be
so	one	and	may
tall.	No	maize.	I

Amy Ludwig VanDerwater

Tip
Use a thesaurus to add to your ideas.

warning drops
soft   *darts*
splinters   *rain*   *sky*
falling   *clattering*

Session 5 Have fun with words

2 Now write a string poem! String together your favourite words creatively to build an image of the topic visually and verbally. The words can be any size and go in any direction.

Ah, I get it! "String them together" – so it's a string poem!

pit...pat...pitter patter...spitter...spatter...splinter...splintering...splattering...showering...clattering...shattering...downpour...deluge!

3 Work with a talk partner to check and edit your string poems. Give each other tips and ideas on how to improve your work.

4 Display final copies of your string poems for everyone to enjoy.

6 Laugh with limericks

A Limericks are short, humorous nonsense poems with a fixed format. Read and enjoy these limericks.

Any volunteers? Who'd like to read out the first one? It's a tongue twister!

A tutor who tooted the flute
Tried to tutor two tooters to toot.
Said the two to the tutor,
"Is it harder to toot or
To tutor two tooters to toot?"
Carolyn Wells

Jeremy, Jeremy Bishop,
Was a good boy, he ate all his fishop.
When he was done,
Like a well-brought up son,
He washed and dried his dishop.
Valerie Bloom

Unit 6 Words at play

Glenelg puts a smile on my face,
With the sea and the sun and the space.
Wish it was my home,
It's a fine palindrome.
Spelled backward it's still the same place.

Jim Haynes

B A limerick has a characteristic pattern of syllables and stresses, or **metre**.

> **metre** *n.* rhythmical patterns of stressed or unstressed syllables in poetry

Tip

Try to work out the typical rhythm of a limerick by saying the syllables to yourself like this: *da DUM da da DUM da da DUM …*

1 What do the three limericks have in common?
   a How many lines are there?
   b How many beats are there in each line?
   c What is the rhyme scheme?
   d What is the common purpose?
2 Suggest three main ingredients that make up a limerick.

C In groups of five, make up a group limerick.
1 Suggest different topics and agree on one as a group.
2 Follow the instructions on page 108 to write your group limerick. Make up a line each.
3 Share your group limerick with the class.

Tip

Choose imaginary people, objects and places to avoid being personal or hurtful. You could make up your own words if you wish!

Session 6 Laugh with limericks

There once was a ... from ...

A ... who was ...

There was a ... named ...

Writing a group limerick

Line 1
- has **three** stressed beats

Line 2
- rhymes with line 1
- has **three** stressed beats

Line 3
- is a shorter line with **two** stressed beats

Line 4
- is the same length as line 3
- rhymes with line 3
- has the same rhythm as line 3

Line 5
- is the same length as lines 1 and 2
- rhymes with lines 1 and 2
- has the same rhythm as lines 1 and 2

End on a humorous note!

D **Write your own limerick.**
1. Make up your own limerick using any ideas from the group work.
2. Once you have drafted, proofread and redrafted your work, write it out in your neatest joined-up handwriting or using ICT.
3. Create a class limericks book for everyone to enjoy!

How did I do?

- Did I work well in a group to make up a limerick?
- Can I play with words to write a creative poem?

7 A different medium

Picture books are not only for young children. In this unit you'll see that stories and plays can be enjoyed in different media that help the reader to understand and visualise the texts.

Vocabulary to learn and use: Shakespeare, manga, theatre, medium, multimedia, incandescent, Ulysses, cynic, illuminate, bard, extended metaphor

1 All the world's a stage

William Shakespeare

Born: April 1564; died 23rd April 1616
Occupation: playwright, poet
Place of birth and death: Stratford-upon-Avon, England
Nickname: Bard (poet) of Avon
Works: 38 plays (histories, comedies and tragedies), 154 sonnets and 2 epic poems

A William Shakespeare has been the most famous English language playwright for several hundred years. Why do people still enjoy his plays, many of which are now successful films?

1 Read and summarise the biography text above in a short paragraph.

> **Tip**
> Remember to introduce your summary with a topic sentence.

2 What might life have been like in Shakespeare's time?
   a How would Shakespeare have written his plays? Would there have been lots of copies or just one?
   b How do you think actors learned their lines?

Any volunteers? Why do you think plays were popular? What didn't they have?

Session 1 All the world's a stage

Did you know?

Playwrights in Shakespeare's time wrote plays for a particular acting company (troupe) to perform. They protected their plays carefully so that other troupes couldn't use them. Occasionally publishers tried to write down the script as a play was performed, but such copies were not very accurate!

B Plays have a story structure and some special features of their own.

Story structure

- Introduction: set scene and introduce characters
- Plot: build up to problem
- Plot: climax or complication
- Plot: solve problem
- Conclusion: tie up loose ends and reflection

1. Discuss how plays and novels are set out. Use these terms:

   paragraphs   chapters   scenes   acts   stage directions
   prologues   dialogue   characters   setting   plot
   Standard English   punctuation   narrative   genre

2. Scan the extract from Shakespeare's play *Julius Caesar* on page 111 for layout features. Do they match your ideas?

Did you know?

The battle of Philippi was fought over two separate days, 3rd and 23rd October, in 42 BCE.

110   Unit 7 A different medium

Roman leaders Brutus and Cassius discuss when and where to take their army into battle against Mark Antony's army to try to win control of the Roman Empire.

Julius Caesar Act 4 Scene 3: Brutus's tent.

BRUTUS: Well, to our work alive. What do you think
Of marching to Philippi presently?

CASSIUS: I do not think it good.

BRUTUS: Your reason?

CASSIUS: This it is:
'Tis better that the enemy seek us,
So shall he waste his means, weary his soldiers,
Doing himself offence; whilst we, lying still,
Are full of rest, defence, and nimbleness.

BRUTUS: Good reasons must of force give place to better:
The people 'twixt Philippi and this ground
Do stand but in a forced affection,
For they have grudged us contribution.
The enemy, marching along by them,
By them shall make a fuller number up,
Come on refreshed, new added, and encouraged,
From which advantage shall we cut him off
If at Philippi we do face him there,
These people at our back.

CASSIUS: Hear me, good brother.

BRUTUS: Under your pardon. You must note beside
That we have tried the utmost of our friends,
Our legions are brimful, our cause is ripe;
The enemy increaseth every day,
We, at the height, are ready to decline.
There is a tide in the affairs of men
Which, taken at the flood, leads on to fortune;
Omitted, all the voyage of their life
Is bound in shallows and in miseries.
On such a full sea are we now afloat,
And we must take the current when it serves
Or lose our ventures.

CASSIUS: Then with your will go on,
We'll along ourselves and meet them at Philippi.

legions *n.pl.* army

2 What has changed?

A 📖 💬 AZ Language is not fixed; words, spelling and punctuation change over time. We don't talk like Shakespeare any more!

1. Talk about words and expressions common to where you live. Would English speakers all over the world know these words and expressions or are they 'local colour'?
2. Which words in the extract look difficult or old-fashioned? Compare your words with a talk partner's and try to work out their meaning from the context.
3. Two contractions are underlined in the text.
   a. What contraction do we use today instead of *'tis*?
   b. *'Twixt* is a contraction for which **archaic** word meaning 'between'?

   > **archaic** *adj.* ancient and no longer in use

   > ### Did you know?
   > Shakespeare didn't always spell his name the same way! Until recently, even dictionaries didn't agree on how to spell the adjective *Shakespearean*. (*Shakespearian? Shaksperean? Shaksperian?*)

4. Which two words make up the compound adjective *brimful*? What do you notice about the spelling of the suffix? What word class are the two original words?
   a. What similar-style adjectives could you form from these words?

   > thank use help law tear forget
   > delight colour power boast disgrace

   b. Choose two or three of the adjectives and use them in sentences.
5. What word ending in modern English would you use instead of *increaseth*? Use the context to help you work it out.
6. Talk about the following as a class and be prepared to offer your views.
   - Do you think people spoke like this every day or just in a play?
   - How do you think dramatising or reading Shakespeare with expression can help understand the unfamiliar language?

   > Well, 'tis clear the Bard like me speaketh not – that scampish pribbling fustilarian!

3 Using language

A Shakespeare is famous for his use of figurative language.

1 Read this extract closely. Brutus uses an *extended metaphor*. Use the plain words version to explain what you think this means.

Original words

There is a tide in the affairs of men
Which, taken at the flood,
leads on to fortune;
Omitted, all the voyage of their life
Is bound in shallows and in miseries.

Plain words

Life is a bit like the tide: if you take advantage when things are flowing well, it leads to good fortune.
If you ignore these opportunities, throughout the voyage of your life you will be trapped in shallow water, and be miserable.

2 In your notebook, write a plain words version of these lines.

On such a full sea are we now afloat,
And we must take the current when it serves
Or lose our ventures.

3 Do these lines extend the sea metaphor or bring in new images?

B Using colons and semicolons.

1 Rewrite these sentences using a colon to add emphasis.
   a John is a brilliant soccer player at our local club.
   b Achim tasted mint and lemon flavours strongly in the drink.
2 How is a colon most commonly used in a play script?

Language focus

A colon introduces: a speaker, a list, an idea or an explanation:
We have many gadgets: televisions, tablets, laptops and smart phones.
We have cancelled tonight's production: the lead actor is sick.
A colon is especially useful for adding emphasis to part of a sentence:
I enjoy one subject the most: English.

3   Rewrite these sentences adding in a semicolon.
   a   The crossword winners were D Davids, 6C R Rutti, 6B and B Dedryver, 6F.
   b   My mother believes in sensible exercise namely, walking and running.
   c   Francois is a talented singer he has won a gold medal.

> **Language focus**
>
> A semicolon creates a break – more than a comma, less than a full stop. It's used to add variety by joining short sentences.
> - It can join two closely related main clauses without a connective: *Bring your reading book tomorrow; you will need it in first period.*
> - It is used before a connective (e.g. *namely, however, therefore, for example, finally, on the other hand*) when it introduces a complete sentence: *You will need to bring some money; however, don't bring too much.*
> - It separates list items where a comma might cause confusion: *The school has students from Paris, France; Tehran, Iran; and Lima, Peru.*

4   *Brutus was in favour of marching to Philippi to fight; Cassius argued that they would win more easily if they stayed where they were.* Why do you think this sentence has a semicolon and not a full stop or a comma?

5   Join different combinations of sentences from the box with a semicolon to form longer sentences.

   Example: *We are going on a journey; my family are all going, including Granny.*

> We are going on a journey.   My brother gets sick on car journeys.
> We are going to the coast.   I will have to pack carefully.
> I must remember to pack a holiday book.
> My family are all going, including Granny.   I am really looking forward to it.
> Mum says to take only a small bag.   I have never been to the seaside before.

> **Tip**
>
> Try to include some of these connectives: *therefore, although, because, however, so, as, but, whereas.*

4 Shakespeare alive

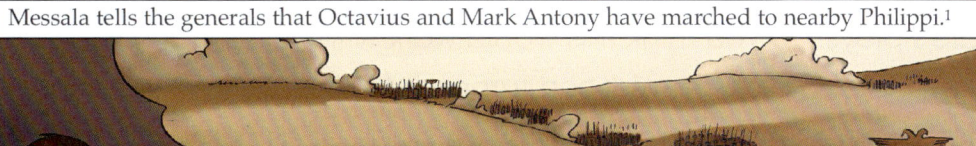

Messala tells the generals that Octavius and Mark Antony have marched to nearby Philippi.[1]

The battlefield is sparse and desolate.

'Tis better that the enemy seek us, so shall he waste his means,[2] weary his soldiers.

Cassius wants to wait for their enemy to come to them.

The people 'twixt[3] Philippi and this ground do stand but in a forced affection.[4]

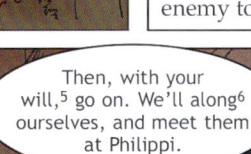

Then, with your will,[5] go on. We'll along[6] ourselves, and meet them at Philippi.

Canst thou hold up thy heavy eyes awhile, and touch thy instrument a strain or two?[7]

However, Brutus believes it is best to head to Philippi first. Cassius concedes to his brother-in-law, and says goodnight.

Brutus calls for his trusted soldiers to keep him company.

Gentle knave,[8] good night. I will not do thee so much wrong to wake thee.

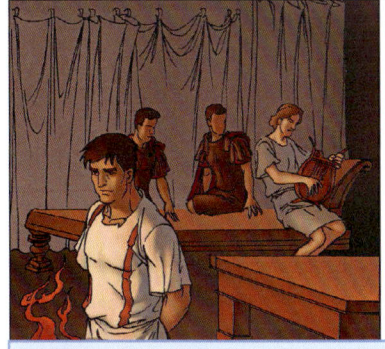

[1] **Philippi** a place in present-day northern Greece
[2] **waste his means** use up his supplies
[3] **'twixt** between
[4] **do stand ... affection** are allies only because they fear us (Brutus is worried they will go over to Mark Antony's side)
[5] **with your will** as you wish
[6] **along** march

Session 4 Shakespeare alive

A 🗨 📖 **Read a modern version of Shakespeare.**

1 Some modern directors change the location or the historical period of Shakespeare's plays. Do you think this would work with *Julius Caesar*?
2 Many Shakespearean plays have been turned into films. Do you think you would prefer to see a Shakespearean play on stage or as a film? Do you think a different format can make something easier to visualise?
3 On page 115, skim over the same scene (Act 4 Scene 3) from *Julius Caesar* in a different format.
   a What genre is this format?
   b What features does it have that the play script did not? Is it easier for you to understand?
   c How is narrative shown?
4 Why do you think some of the original words have been kept?

B 🗨 📝 **Write an opinion paragraph comparing the versions.**

1 As a preparation for your paragraph, talk in a group.
   a What similarities and differences are there between the play script and the graphic version?
   b How does the format affect how you read the text?
   c What do you think of Shakespeare's writing? Suggest reasons why people still enjoy his plays.
2 Write a paragraph comparing the formats. Explain which version you prefer.
3 Add *Julius Caesar* to your learning journal and note down your thoughts about the different versions.

> **Tip**
>
> Start an opinion paragraph with a topic sentence summarising your view. Then give details of your ideas with examples, and conclude your argument.

How did I do?
- Did I identify features of play scripts?
- Did I understand that language has changed over time?
- Did I compare two versions of a play?

Unit 7 A different medium

5 Introducing manga!

A 📖 💬 Manga are Japanese comic books. Their distinctive style was developed in Japan over 100 years ago!

Did you know?

Manga are very popular in Japan; adults as well as children read them. Manga come in lots of genres, from action-adventure to science fiction, historical stories and even business!

Contents

Chapter 1 3
Chapter 2 79
Chapter 3 119
Afterword 157

NO.6 VOLUME ONE

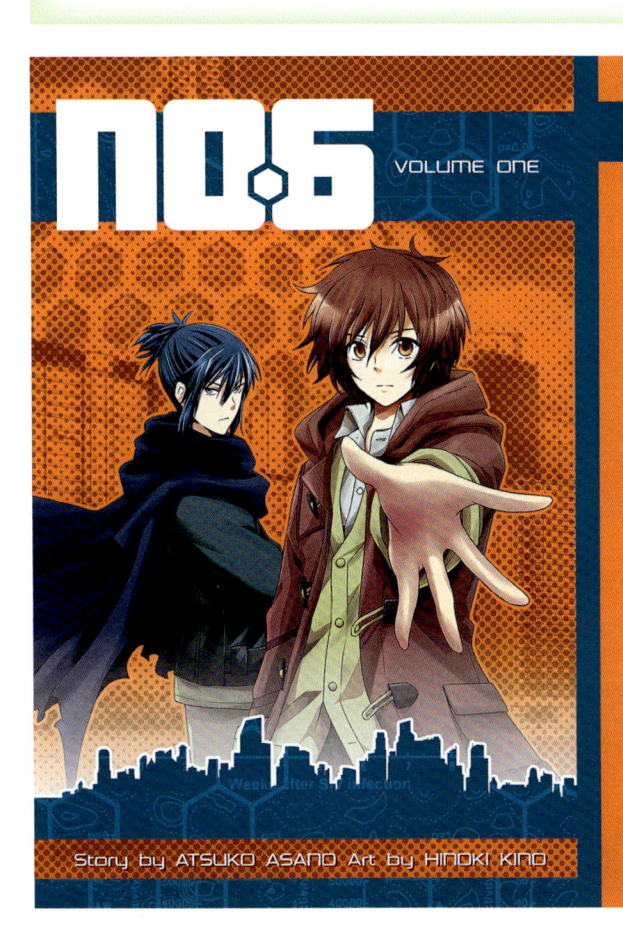

Story by ATSUKO ASANO Art by HINOKI KINO

A PERFECT LIFE, IN A PERFECT CITY

Shion, an elite student living in an exclusive area of technologically advanced city No. 6, leads a carefully managed life. Selected at the age of 2, Shion knows no different until his 12th birthday – the day he takes in the injured Rat, a fugitive from the raging typhoon outside and from the city's special security services; Rat is definitely not a member of the elite. Deciding to help Rat is a decision that brings chaos to Shion's carefully ordered world and threatens to reveal the secrets behind City No. 6.

1. **a** Look at the manga book cover. What is the title of the series?
   b Where does this book come in the series? How can you tell?
   c Who are the main characters? What can you find out about them?
2. Compare the manga cover with the cover of one of your books when it is opened out. Which way does the manga book open up? What does this suggest about the pages inside?

3 What clues tell you the genre?

4 Are you surprised that this book is divided into chapters? Why?

5 What do you think an *Afterword* is?

6 Does the story setting seem exciting?

> **Tip**
>
> Check your answer in **Book talk** on page 175.

B 📖 💬 **The manga tells the story through a cartoon strip.**

1 What is unusual about how you read the frames in this extract?

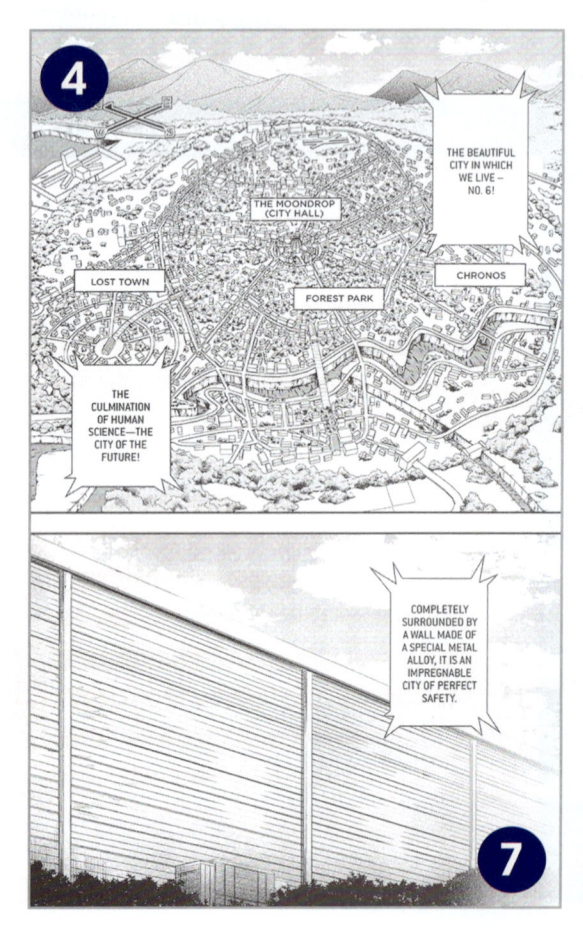

Unit 7 A different medium

2. Suggest why different shaped text boxes are used.
3. Shion is the narrator as well as a character. Which frame contains narrative text told by him? How can you tell?
4. a Where is Shion's mother?
   b How is she speaking? What tells you this?
   c Give two reasons why she might be speaking that way.
   d What does Shion call her? What does this suggest about their relationship?
5. Why is Shion looking backwards in frame 1?
6. Why is he drawn so much smaller in frame 2?
7. In frame 6, what do the faces imply about the people?

6 Shion

A A picture of Shion is beginning to emerge.

1. Plan a character profile about Shion as a mind map. Use the questions below and add more of your own. Note examples from the text and cover.

   - How old is he?
   - How is he dressed?
   - What does an 'unrestricted life' mean?
   - How does he speak?
   - Does he seem happy?
   - What do his gestures, movement and expression tell you?
   - Is Shion a good person?

2. Shion goes on to help Rat, a fugitive from the authorities. Does that seem in or out of character?
3. Write three paragraphs about Shion:
   - paragraph 1: his lifestyle and home – descriptive
   - paragraph 2: his personality – descriptive
   - paragraph 3: why Shion helps Rat – your opinion.

> **Tip**
> Include examples from the text. Use connectives to link the ideas in your opinion paragraph.

Session 6 Shion

7 Standard format

A What difference would it make if the No.6 story had been written as a novel with a prologue, narrative and dialogue?

1 Plan a rewrite of the extract in the format of a novel.
   a Which parts would you turn into the prologue? Why?
   b Who would narrate the novel? Shion or a third person?
2 Rewrite the extract according to your plan.
   a Make any necessary changes to make the text fit the new format.
   b Check your dialogue punctuation.
   c Include suitable headings for the prologue and the chapter.

> **Tip**
> Remember to start a new line for each new speaker.

3 Compare your rewrite with a talk partner's and discuss the differences.

8 Medium makes a difference

A It's good to know what you like and why.

1 Think about your opinion of different media.
   - Which was easier to read: the original Shakespeare text or the graphic novel version?
   - Did you prefer No.6 as a graphic novel or in your rewritten version?
   - Do you feel the same about all books?
2 Prepare a two-minute presentation on your opinion of different media.
   - Describe the different media you have read in this unit.
   - Suggest how different media can be used in the classroom.
   - Give your view on which medium you prefer and why.

9 A multimedia novel

A 📖 👥 So far in this unit you have studied a play, a graphic novel and a Japanese manga book. The text you'll look at in this session combines media formats.

1. Kate DiCamillo's novel *Flora and Ulysses: The Illuminated Adventures* is 'interspersed with comic-style graphic sequences and full-page illustrations'. What do you think this means? Does it sound like something you would enjoy?
2. Skim over the opening of the book on page 122 and see what you think.
3. In pairs, read the dialogue aloud, using body language and expression. Imagine each character's feelings about the vacuum cleaner.
4. In your own words, summarise the cartoon sequence.
5. Would you describe the cartoon sequence as a prologue or a preface? Why?
6. What do you think began with a vacuum cleaner?

> **Tip**
> Check you know what prologues and prefaces are in **Book talk** on page 175.

B 💬 📝 Practise your narrative and dialogue skills. Work in pairs.

Write out the cartoon sequence in narrative form with dialogue.

- Use the exact words for the dialogue, punctuated correctly.
- Write the narrative in the third person, in the past tense. Explain what is going on in the Tickham household.
- Choose precise, descriptive words in place of *said* to show the speaker's actions and feelings. Here are some you could use.

> screeched laughed glowered glared babbled gulped
> pondered snapped snorted agreed squeaked beamed
> tempted blurted boasted exclaimed explained wailed
> groaned sighed pleaded grumbled muttered reasoned
> insisted stormed pointed out conceded continued

Session 9 A multimedia novel

Flora and Ulysses: The Illuminated Adventures

Flora Buckman and her family live next door to the Tickhams. It is Mrs Tickham's birthday.

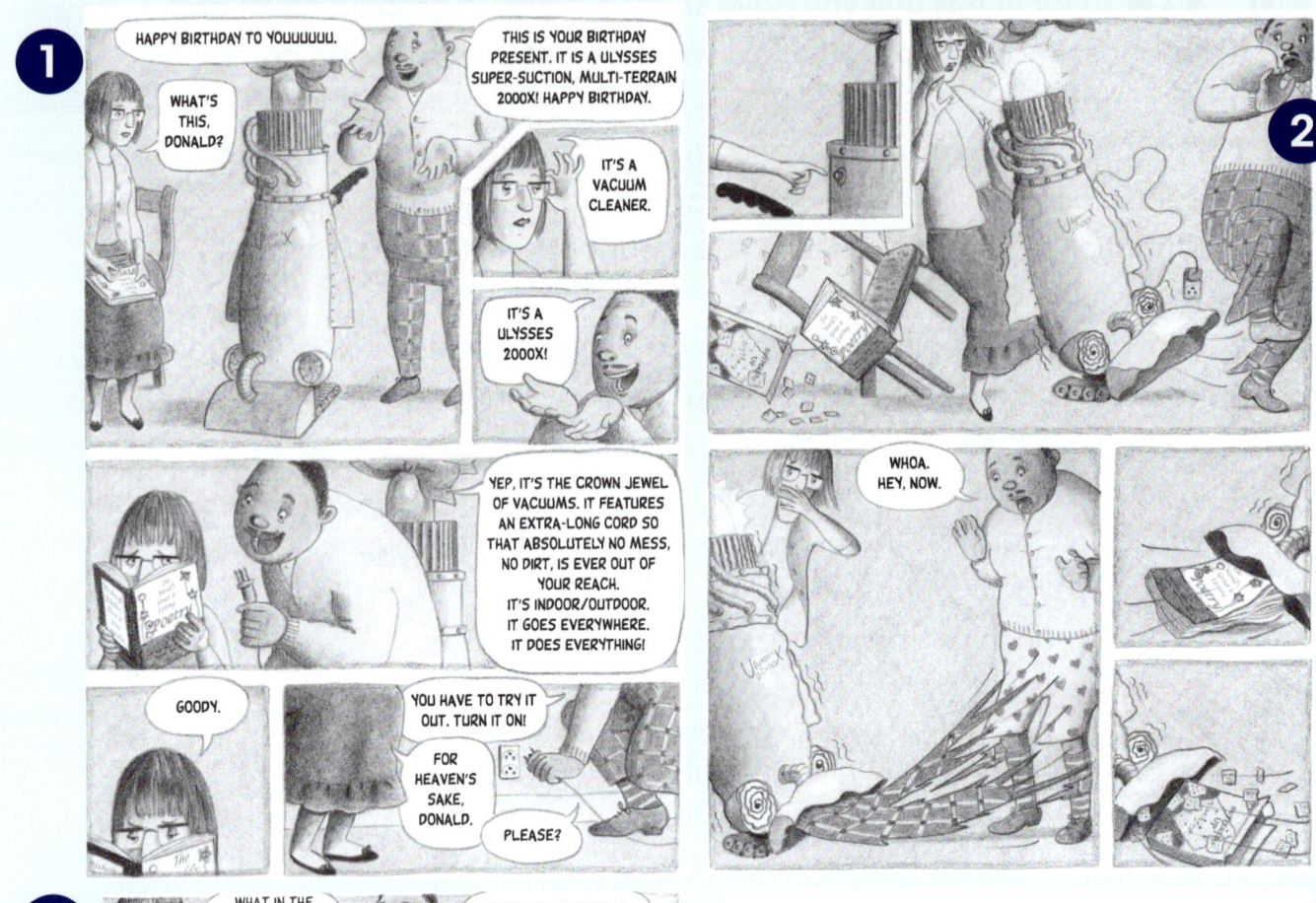

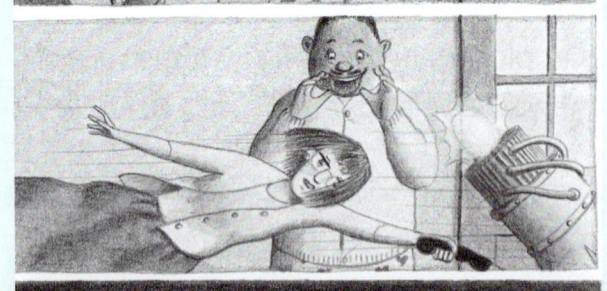

1

HAPPY BIRTHDAY TO YOUUUUUU.

WHAT'S THIS, DONALD?

THIS IS YOUR BIRTHDAY PRESENT. IT IS A ULYSSES SUPER-SUCTION, MULTI-TERRAIN 2000X! HAPPY BIRTHDAY.

IT'S A VACUUM CLEANER.

IT'S A ULYSSES 2000X!

YEP, IT'S THE CROWN JEWEL OF VACUUMS. IT FEATURES AN EXTRA-LONG CORD SO THAT ABSOLUTELY NO MESS, NO DIRT, IS EVER OUT OF YOUR REACH. IT'S INDOOR/OUTDOOR. IT GOES EVERYWHERE. IT DOES EVERYTHING!

GOODY.

YOU HAVE TO TRY IT OUT. TURN IT ON!

FOR HEAVEN'S SAKE, DONALD. PLEASE?

2

WHOA. HEY, NOW.

3

WHAT IN THE WORLD, DONALD?

IT'S MULTI-TERRAIN! YOU SHOULD TRY IT OUTSIDE!

AND THAT'S HOW IT ALL BEGAN. WITH A VACUUM CLEANER. REALLY.

4

CHAPTER ONE
A Natural-Born Cynic

Flora Belle Buckman was in her room at her desk. She was very busy. She was doing two things at once. She was ignoring her mother, and she was also reading a comic book entitled *The Illuminated Adventures of the Amazing Incandesto!*

"Flora," her mother shouted, "what are you doing up there?"

"I'm reading!" Flora shouted back.

"Remember the contract!" her mother shouted. "Do not forget the contract!"

At the beginning of summer, in a moment of weakness, Flora had made the mistake of signing a contract that said she would "work to turn her face away from the idiotic high jinks of comics and towards the bright light of true literature".

Those were the exact words of the contract. They were her mother's words.

Flora's mother was a writer. She was divorced, and she wrote romance novels.

Talk about idiotic high jinks.

Flora hated romance novels.

In fact, she hated romance.

C 💬 📝 **Discuss the questions before answering them in your notebook.**

1. Do you think the events shown in the cartoon sequence take place before or after the beginning of Chapter 1? Why?
2. a What does the vacuum cleaner's name suggest about it?
   b Do you think Ulysses is a good name for a vacuum cleaner?

> **Did you know?**
> Ulysses was an ancient Greek king, warrior and hero who had many exciting adventures.

3. a How can you tell that Flora is one of the main characters?
   b What is she doing when the chapter opens?
4. What do you think the chapter title (*A Natural-Born* **Cynic**) means? Who do you think it refers to?

> **cynic** *n.* a person who believes that people are only interested in themselves and are not sincere

5. a What are the actual words of the contract? How can you tell?
   b What does the contract mean? Why do you think Flora's mother made her sign it?
   c Is Flora obeying the contract? How do you know?
6. What do you think *The Illuminated Adventures of the Amazing Incandesto!* is about? Why?
7. Which meaning of *illuminate* is used in the comic title?
   a to light something
   b to explain something that is difficult to understand
   c to decorate a book with colour, gold paint and small pictures
8. a How can you tell Amazing Incandesto is a name?
   b Look up *incandescent*. What sort of superhero might the Amazing Incandesto be?
9. Why do you think the author includes details of Flora's comic book?

D 💬 **Flora hears a commotion outside in her neighbours' garden.**

1. Which of these sights do you think she sees?
   a The vacuum cleaner dragging Mrs Tickham round the garden.
   b Mrs Tickham vacuuming the yard.

Session 9 A multimedia novel

2 Flora rescues a squirrel from the Tickhams' vacuum cleaner and calls it Ulysses. Do you think the Ulysses in the book's title is the squirrel or the vacuum cleaner? Why?

3 Based on what you have read, predict what turns out to be unusual about the squirrel. Share your ideas in a group.

10 Language matters

A Discuss the narrative style in your group.

1 Which words in the box describe the narrative style of *Flora and Ulysses*? Find examples in the extract to support your choices.

> engaging stiff light-hearted friendly formal
> unusual bossy chatty serious humorous
> dull mysterious formal quirky

2 Does the style of the narrative match the style of the comic strip?

3 Is the narrative in the first or third person? What tells you this?

4 a Does the narrator seem to sympathise with Flora or with her mother? What evidence shows this?

b Use the title of the book to help you decide whether the author shares the narrator's view of Flora and her mother.

c Who do you feel sympathetic towards so far? Why?

Language focus

A new paragraph usually signals a change of action, time, place, idea or speaker. Sometimes a new paragraph is used to emphasise an idea or a few important words.

B 📖 💬 **Paragraphs are as important in fiction as in non-fiction.**

1 a Tell a talk partner the main idea of each paragraph in the extract from Chapter 1 on page 122. Why was each new paragraph started?

b Which reason for starting a new paragraph would not appear in a non-fiction text?

2 Look at the final sentence of the first paragraph (*She was ignoring her mother … the Amazing Incandesto!*). What tells you whether this sentence is a compound or a complex sentence?

3 What is the effect of the short sentences in the final paragraph?

4 Re-read Mr Tickham's longest bit of dialogue (beginning *YEP, IT'S THE …*).

a Is his second sentence a compound or a complex sentence? How can you tell? What is its purpose?

b What is the effect of the short sentences immediately afterwards?

C 📖 📝 **AZ** **Connectives link sentences according to their meaning.**

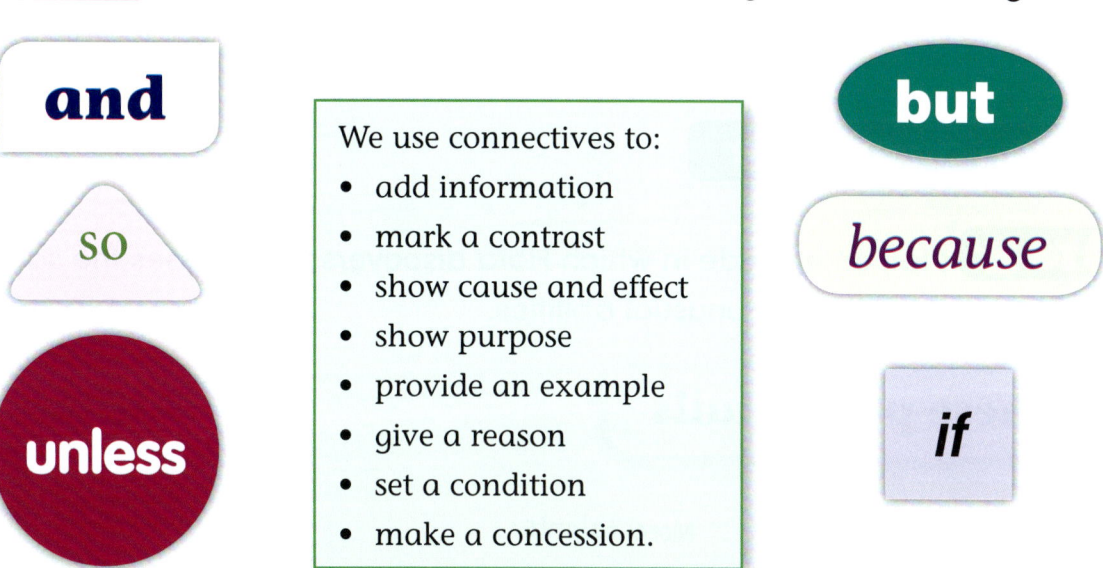

and

so

unless

We use connectives to:
- add information
- mark a contrast
- show cause and effect
- show purpose
- provide an example
- give a reason
- set a condition
- make a concession.

but

because

if

1 Use the box to explain the purpose of the underlined connectives.

a Flora is reading a comic <u>although</u> she agreed not to.

b Comics help us visualise events; <u>in addition</u> they are fun to read.

c <u>As a result of</u> not learning my work, I did not do well in the test.

d I read novels <u>so that</u> I can escape into other people's adventures.

e I really enjoy reading; <u>in particular</u> I enjoy science fiction.

Session 10 Language matters

2 Choose **five** connectives from the box and use them in sentences. Write the purpose of the connective at the end of each sentence.

> although   however   therefore   on the other hand   since   so that
> in order to   in addition   as a result   for example   unless

Tip

Make sure you can spell these connectives – look out for letter patterns and smaller words inside them to help you remember.

D What is your opinion of the mix of comic strips, ordinary narrative and full page illustrations in *Flora and Ulysses*?

1 Summarise points for and against the mixed format, using examples from the extract. Send a spokesperson to present your points to another group
2 Find out another group's points by asking their spokesperson questions.
3 Have a class vote on whether you would read more books like this.

11 Plan an episode

A Plan an episode in which Flora discovers that Ulysses the squirrel has developed some unusual abilities.

Use these plot details

Ulysses' talents:
- can fly
- super strength

More talents:
- writes poetry
- uses typewriter (can't spell!)

Flora must keep Ulysses' talents a secret
- to protect him
- to stop him flying!

Mother finds empty chip packets by typewriter – accuses Flora

Flora finds an unusual, badly spelled poem

Unit 7 A different medium

1. Copy this storyboard into your notebook. Add plot details for each paragraph. Think of words to use and jot them down.

Paragraph 1	Paragraph 2	Paragraph 3	Paragraph 4
Flora finds something unusual	She finds more clues	Flora sees Ulysses do something amazing	Both are surprised
Paragraph 5	**Paragraph 6**	**Paragraph 7**	
Flora's mother almost finds out	Flora saves the day	Conclusion: makes you want to read on	

2. Decide which paragraph you could make into a cartoon sequence. What sort of exclamations might Flora or her mother use?

12 Make and display a final copy

A Write and illustrate your chapter.

1. Base your chapter on your planning. Include:
   - an exciting or quirky chapter title
   - a cartoon sequence
   - a similar narrative style to the novel
   - third person narrative
   - dialogue
   - a cliff-hanger ending to make you want to read on!
2. Design a creative layout for your chapter.

> What do you think a *cliff-hanger* ending is? Think about the visual image it conjures up!

Tip

You could use ICT to create a full multimedia chapter.

3. Proofread and revise your work to improve the style and choice of words.
4. Make a class display of all the chapters.

How did I do?

- Did I identify features of multimedia novels?
- Did I tell a story through words and pictures?
- Did I match the same style as Chapter 1?

8 Make it happen

In this unit you'll find out about some interesting ways to recycle and will read an article about someone who has put a good idea into action. You'll follow instructions to make something out of recycled materials and have a chance to write a report on recycling in your school.

Vocabulary to learn and use: reduce, reuse, recycle, sustainable, magazine, tyre, sequence

1 Weighing up waste

A Humans generate an enormous amount of waste.

1 How much waste do you think you create?

- How much waste does your family create in one day?
- What do you do with your waste?
- Where does your waste go? What happens to it?
- Do you collect and reuse any of your waste?

2 Look at some of these ideas for what you can do with waste! Which ideas do you like the most? Do you know of any other **novel** ideas?

novel *adj.* new or different

Handbags made from sweet wrappers

A chandelier made from plastic bottles

A bag made from a football

Unit 8 Make it happen

3 Do you think making, buying and using recycled products is a good idea?
   a In groups, discuss points for and against these statements.

   > It's better to use recycled products.

   > Recycled goods aren't necessarily better or cheaper.

   b Choose a spokesperson to summarise and present your group's points of view to the class.

B **The prefix re can be attached to almost any verb to change its meaning.**

1 Rewrite these words with the prefix **re** added to the front of the word.

   wash   supply   attach   charge   teach   play

2 What does **re** mean in the context of these words? Use a dictionary to check your answer.
3 Give other examples of verbs where the prefix **re** has the same meaning. List the words in your notebook with their definitions.
4 Sometimes a hyphen is used if the other word begins with *e* e.g. *re-elect*.
   Find other examples in your dictionary.

> **Any volunteers?**
> Sometimes *re* is used as an abbreviation for a word meaning 'in connection with'. What is this word?

2 Read a magazine article

A **Read and understand a magazine article on the next page about someone who uses recycling to make a difference in her community.**

1 Who is the article about and what is the main recycled material?
2 Work out a definition for the three underlined terms from the context. Then check your ideas using a dictionary.
3 Find two synonyms in the text for the word *global*.
4 A proper noun that is used as an adjective is called a proper adjective e.g. *African* in the phrase *an African businesswoman*. Find two other proper adjectives in the text and write them out with their related nouns.

The sole of the matter

Bethlehem Alemu, founder and managing director of soleRebels Footwear, is making a difference by creating jobs and hope out of old car tyres!

In 2004, Bethlehem Tilahun Alemu left her ordinary accountancy job and started making shoes! Today, her company soleRebels is Africa's largest footwear brand, with her shoes selling in over 50 countries worldwide.

Alemu is one of Africa's most celebrated businesswomen. She has featured on the front cover of magazines and was selected as a "Young Global Leader" by the World Economic Forum 2011. She has even won the award for "Most Outstanding Businesswoman" at the annual African Business Awards.

You may be wondering about the secret to her success. Well, it's no secret! Her enthusiasm is **contagious** as she describes how her success is based on creating jobs by making use of local skills, natural resources and business opportunities. Bethlehem describes how she came up with her brainchild.

"Having grown up in a small village (near Addis Ababa), watching our family and neighbours struggling, we decided to create the 'better life' we were all waiting for by harnessing our community's incredible **artisan** skills and channelling them into a **sustainable**, global, fair trade footwear business."

soleRebels Footwear includes sandals, flip flops and shoes with soles made from recycled car tyres. Her designs use recycled and sustainable materials with hand-spun organic cotton fabrics, and natural fibres including pure Abyssinian **koba**!

"We took this wonderful indigenous age-old recycling tradition and fused it with fantastic Ethiopian crafts and modern design and turned it into footwear with universal flavour and appeal."

You are sure to catch a sparkle in her eye as she concludes, "Our motto at soleRebels is: 'Making the world a better place, one step at a time'. So have fun, help others and be proud that you are making the world a better place. What more could you ask from your shoes?"

---

contagious *adj.* infectious
artisan *n.* a skilled, manual worker
sustainable *adj.* something that keeps going and maintains itself
koba *n.* a plant that is indigenous to Ethiopia

Any volunteers?
Why do you think the name 'soleRebels' is spelled in lower case with a capital letter in the middle?

Did you know?

The koba plant (or Ethiopian banana) is a unique natural resource because every part of the tree has a use – from shade and jewellery to building materials and food. It symbolises local sustainability!

5 Based on the article, how would you describe Bethlehem Alemu? Use three or four adjectives.
6 What inspired her to start a company?
7 What is her motto?
8 What is the 'secret' to her success?

B Paragraphs are useful. They help to organise a text, contain main ideas and separate the dialogue from information or narrative.

1 How many paragraphs does this article have?
2 What is the main idea of each paragraph? Summarise each paragraph in one sentence.

> **Tip**
> Remember that a lead sentence or paragraph tells us who, what, where, when, why and how.

3 What word in the last paragraph shows that the article is ending?
4 Is the order important? Would the information still make sense if the paragraphs were ordered differently?

C To grasp a play on a word you need to understand its original meaning.

1 Basing your ideas on the definitions in the box, what does the name 'soleRebels' imply? Do you think it is a good name for a shoe company?
2 Explain the play on the word *sole* in the title of the article.
3 What expressions do you know that use the word *sole* or *soul*? How would you use these expressions in a sentence?

Session 2 Read a magazine article 131

3 Compare texts

A 📖 💬 📝 **Discuss the features of a magazine article.**

Title ✓
Lead
By-line
Columns
Paragraphs

1 Make a list of magazine article features. Leave space for your list to grow.
2 Use your list to compare the magazine article features with the features of the news reports in Units 2 and 5. Tick features that are similar. Put a question mark, cross or comment next to any that are different.
3 How are their purpose and style different?

> **Tip**
> Think about what you expect from a newspaper or magazine. Which do you prefer to read? Why?

4 Find two examples in the soleRebels article where the reader is addressed in the second person narrative (*you*).
5 Write a short paragraph describing the features of a magazine article.

B 💬 **Recall the features of a biography.**

1 Decide which statements are true about a biography.

> a It is an account of someone's life written by someone else in the third person narrative.
> b It includes facts about the person's background, history and accomplishments.
> c It includes quotations.
> d It is written from the writer's point of view and has a particular tone.
> e It is written in the past and sometimes the present tense.

2 In what way is the magazine article a type of biography?
3 Find an example of sentences written in the past and present tenses.
4 Why is the article not written in the future tense?
5 Make up a sentence using the future tense to add to the article.

4 Revise punctuation

A Journalists have to use correct and effective punctuation because their work is in the public eye. Analyse the punctuation in the text.

Any volunteers? Can you explain what 'in the public eye' means?

1. Give two different ways that capitalisation is used in the text.
2. Explain why brackets are used in the first sentence of Paragraph 5:
   'Having grown up in a small village (near Addis Ababa) …'

Language focus

Speech marks are also called quotation marks or inverted commas.
They can be single (' … ') or double (" … ") and can be used to indicate:
- direct speech
- someone's quoted words
- a title
- figurative speech or colloquial speech.

3. **a** Find an example of a quotation in the magazine article.
   b Why are speech marks used round "Young Global Leader" and "Most Outstanding Businesswoman"?
   c What is the 'better life' referring to? Why is it in speech marks?
4. **a** What is the purpose of the exclamation mark in these sentences?
   - In 2004, Bethlehem Tilahun Alemu left her ordinary accountancy job and started making shoes!
   - Well, it's no secret!
   - Her designs use … natural fibres including pure Abyssinian koba!

   b As a general rule, exclamations are not used in formal writing; what does this tell you about the style of this text?
5. Find two hyphenated words. Explain the purpose of the hyphen.
6. Explain the use of the comma in each of the following:
   - … channelling them into a sustainable, global, fair trade, footwear business.
   - Today, her company soleRebels is Africa's largest footwear brand.

Session 4 Revise punctuation 133

B In pairs, prepare a short biographical paragraph on each other for a school magazine.

1. Interview your talk partner to find out about something that has made them proud or happy e.g. an achievement at school, an award, a family event like having a new baby brother or sister, or being a good recycler. Take notes using key words. Record some quotations that you can use.
2. Write a first draft, using the list of features from the previous session to guide you.
3. Ask your talk partner to check that your first draft has the correct details. Make sure they agree with what you've written about them.
4. Edit your paragraph and keep it for a class writing activity later on.

How did I do?

- Did I read and understand a magazine article?
- Did I compare the features of magazine articles and news reports?
- Can I write a biographical paragraph?

5 Follow instructions

A Skim the text on the next page and talk about the features.

1. What is familiar about the layout?
2. What is the purpose of the text? Who is it for?
3. Is the sequence of the information important? Why?
4. What is the purpose of the diagrams?

B Read for detail and understand the text.

1. What is the theme and function of the shoe?
2. When will you need an adult's help?
3. What is a 'paddle shape'?
4. What materials can be recycled to make these shoes?
5. Would this shoe be effective in a rainstorm? Why?
6. Are the instructions clear? How could you improve them?

Sahara sand shoes

You need

A sharp pencil, scissors, ruler, glue
Thick and thin pieces of cardboard
Two shoelaces or string
Four old buttons with large holes
Paint and paintbrush
A nail to make holes in the cardboard

What to do

1 Trace the shape of each foot onto thick cardboard. Make a 'paddle shape' around each pattern to create extra space around the edges of your foot.
2 Ask an adult to help you cut out four shapes for each foot from the thick cardboard. Cut four strips (about 5 cm wide and 10 cm long) from thinner cardboard for shoe straps.
3 For each shoe, glue four paddle shapes together with the ends of the shoe straps glued between the top two layers. The straps should be on each side of the shoe and angled toward the toes.
4 Paint designs on the shoes.
5 Place your feet on the soles and draw a line between your big toe and second toe. Ask an adult to make two holes on each end of the lines.
6 Fold the straps inward so they cross over the holes in the sole and punch two holes through the crossed straps.
7 For each shoe, thread a shoelace through the straps and the sole from the top to the bottom, in and out of a button, and back to the top through the other hole.
8 Thread the shoelace through a second button at the top. Put the shoes on and slide the top button down until the shoes fit securely on your feet. Then tie the shoelace and off you go!

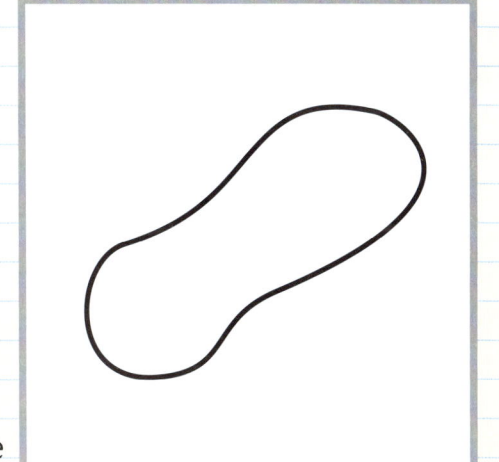

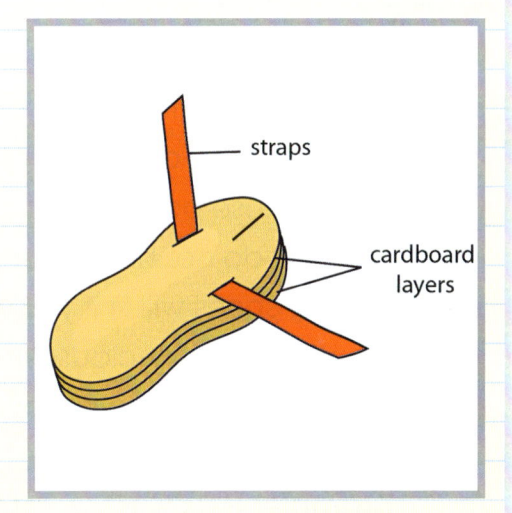

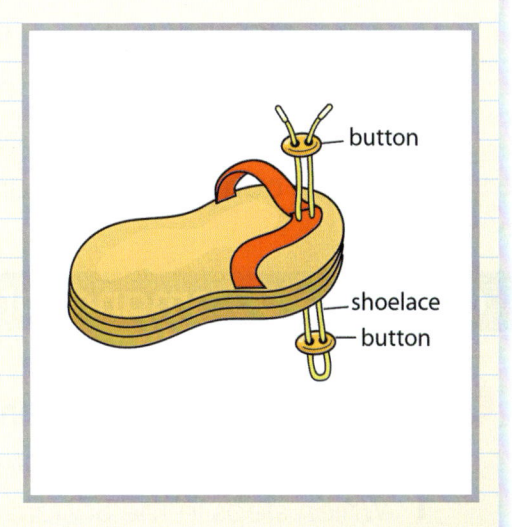

Session 5 Follow instructions

C 📖 ✏️ A conditional clause in a sentence helps clarify an instruction. It is also called the *If* clause.

> **Language focus**
>
> A conditional sentence (*If* clause + main clause) expresses possibility. It expresses something that may possibly happen in the future, or might have happened in the past, as a result of a particular condition or circumstance. The *If* clause can go before the main clause or after it.
>
> *If I listen, I will understand.*
>
> *I will understand if I listen.*

1 These sentences can be added to the instructions for making sand shoes. Where do you think they belong?
  a You'll need a strong pair of scissors if the cardboard is very thick.
  b If you use paint, you should wait until it is dry before continuing.
  c If you do not have shoelaces, you can use string.
  d Your shoes will fit if you've measured correctly.

2 Identify the main clause in the sentences above.

3 Add a main clause or conditional clause to complete the following sentences:

  Example: *If you wear these shoes in the rain, they will break.*
  a If you'd like to change the style, …
  b If there is no adult to help you, …
  c You can use other materials if …
  d You can use an old cardboard box if …

6 Use the command form

A 📖 ✏️ Instructions use command verbs to tell the reader what to do.

Example: *Read the instructions carefully.*

1 Which steps in the Sahara sand shoes text begin with a command verb?
2 Write three of your own examples in your notebook and underline the command verb in the sentences.

Language focus

A command verb gives an order e.g. Complete the task is actually (You) complete the task.
The word *you* is not mentioned but it is understood to be the subject.
A modifier can be added to tell you how, why or when to do the action:
Before you complete the task, wash your hands.

B **Connectives are used in instructions to join two commands.**

1. Choose the best connective to join the following commands. Include the subject (if you need to) when you join the sentences.

   Example: Ask an adult to help you. Use sharp scissors. (when/although)
   Ask an adult to help you when you use sharp scissors.

   a. Collect the materials together. Begin the task. (as/before)
   b. Keep your foot still. Trace the pattern (while/until)
   c. Stir the paint. Add the water. (as/before)
   d. Wait a while. The paint is dry. (until/by the time)

Language focus

Connectives link phrases, clauses and sentences. They can extend complex sentences to add clarity where necessary.
Wait for ten minutes while the paint dries before you continue to decorate the shoes.

2. Circle the connectives in these complex sentences. Do they occur in the same place in each sentence?

   Example: (When) the paint is dry, add your designs (before) you wear them.

   a. Mix the paint while the glue is drying in order to save time.
   b. Once you've drawn the pattern, cut the cardboard, but ask an adult to help you with this.
   c. Finally, punch holes in the cardboard so you can thread the lace and tie it together.
   d. Once they are at an angle, cut the strips out, then glue them together.

3 Read the sentences in the previous activity to a talk partner. Use the correct expression, demonstrating the pause and emphasis in each one.

C Do you remember how to use a semicolon? Read the information in the **Language focus** box to help you revise.

> ### Language focus
>
> A semicolon creates a break – more than a comma, less than a full stop. It can be used with or in place of a connective and creates a pause between two equally important ideas without starting a new sentence: *She lost the directions; she made it home safely.*

1. Read these instructions aloud. Identify the pause in each one.
2. Rewrite the sentences in your notebook with a semicolon placed correctly.
   a. Shoes made from cardboard will be fine in sand they will not work well in the rain.
   b. It is better to use thin cardboard it's easier to cut.
   c. Liquid glue works well it's the best glue for the job.
   d. Thick cardboard may be difficult to cut ask an adult for help.

7 Create your own design

A Invent your own pair of homemade shoes from recycled materials and give a demonstration to the class.

1. Choose a theme for your shoes. Use one of these ideas or an idea of your own.

   - celebrate spring
   - space shoes for Mars
   - deep sea diving flippers
   - a practical invention
   - anti-mud shoes

2. Draw a simple diagram to plan your design.
3. Make the shoes at home or in class.
4. Use the shoes and diagram to tell the class how you made them.
5. Remember to speak clearly!

Unit 8 Make it happen

B Write a set of instructions on how to make your unique shoes using only recycled materials.

1. List the required materials. They should include recycled things like kitchen rolls, boxes, scrap paper and plastic.
2. Write instructions on how to make the shoes. Divide your instructions into between five and ten ordered steps, and use connectives and conditional (*If*) clauses to extend your sentences.
3. Include some diagrams to illustrate a few of the steps.

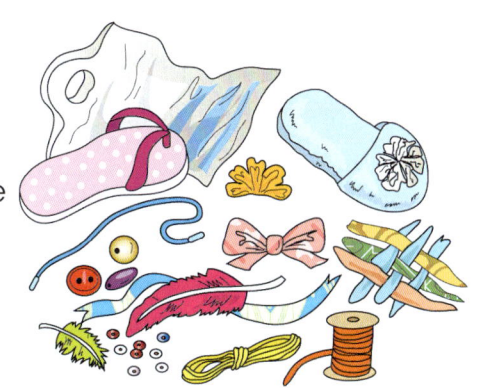

How did I do?

- Did I follow instructions to make a pair of shoes?
- Did I extend sentences using conditional clauses and connectives?
- Can I write my own instructions?

8 Read a non-chronological report

A A report gives information in a formal way. There are different types of reports. Every report has a reason or purpose.

1. Discuss the different purposes of these reports and match them with the sentence examples below.
   - news report
   - balanced report
   - biased report
   - instructional report
   - non-chronological report

> The common garden bee does more than simply make honey.

> Yesterday, bad weather prevented children from attending school.

> While many believe that mobile phones are an essential part of our lives, the negative impacts should be considered.

> Studies show that watching TV is detrimental for young children.

> The following guidelines explain how to run the machine.

Session 8 Read a non-chronological report

B Read a non-chronological report

1 Scan the report on recycling to find examples of these features.

> impersonal style   headings   third person   conclusion
> introduction   visual information   paragraphs   connectives

2 List the underlined terms and work out their meanings by discussing the words in context.

Recycling

Introduction

Recycling has become a <u>'buzz' word</u> for today's generation. Environmentalists are <u>lobbying</u> for people to change their lifestyles and do something about the waste they generate. However, not everyone is aware of this 'war on waste' and many seem unclear what all the fuss is about.

What is recycling?

Recycling means collecting <u>discarded</u> waste and using it to create a different product. Old items can be recycled in different ways. For example, old tyres can be reused whole as road barriers or swings for children, or they can be melted down and the rubber used to make new things such as building materials, tiles and sports surfaces.

Why recycle?

Years ago, before the invention of plastics and other <u>non-biodegradable</u> materials, disposing of waste was less of a concern. Now that people produce so much non-biodegradable waste, it is more difficult to find places to store it.

Much waste is dumped in <u>landfill sites.</u> However, landfill sites take up large areas of land and the waste may remain there for many years – perhaps even centuries – and can pollute the environment. Recycling is an <u>alternative</u> way of dealing with it, reducing the amount of waste in the environment and protecting the planet from pollution.

Recycling is also important in the effort to reduce the amount of new materials used for manufacturing things. This is necessary because there is not an unlimited supply of natural resources and they may run out. Furthermore, it can also be more cost-effective to reuse old materials instead of using new ones. So recycling can help save money!

How to recycle

Awareness and good habits are key to being a responsible recycler. Consumers should always check to see whether a product is recycled or can be recycled by looking for the 'recycling loop'.

The three steps in the recycling process are known as 'the three Rs':

- **Reduce** – Get into the habit of throwing away fewer items and only buy things that you really need, that last a long time or that come with minimal packaging, such as loose fresh produce.

- **Reuse** – Choose products that can be used again (e.g. rechargeable batteries), fix broken products or find new ways to use things. An old container can become a flower pot, for example.

- **Recycle** – Use separate bins to collect and separate different types of waste items and take them to a recycling centre. Remember that some items can't be recycled so it is important to find out how to dispose of them properly. You can't recycle some oil-based liquid cleaners, for example; allow these liquids to solidify before throwing them out or give some to a friend to use.

Conclusion

Recycling is important because it helps to look after the environment. If everyone recycled their waste, much less waste would pollute the environment. Recycling is about looking ahead. If future generations are to have a clean world to live in, free from environmental issues, recycling needs to happen today.

Did you know?

The recycling symbol is used worldwide to mark items that are or can be recycled. The three arrows stand for the three important steps in the recycling process. The symbol was inspired by the Möbius strip.

C Read the report in detail to answer these questions.

1. Is this report written for adults, children or both? How can you tell?
2. What is its purpose?
3. Which word in each pair best describes the language in this text? Use examples from the text to support your choice.

> formal/informal   personal/impersonal
> factual/opinionated   biased/unbiased

4. Is the expression *war on waste* literal or figurative? What does it imply?
5. What does the recycling symbol represent? Explain it in your own words.

Any volunteers?
Why not do some independent research? Find out what the Möbius strip is and who discovered it. Make or draw one and explain how it works to your group.

9 Summarise the report

A Work in groups to summarise the report on recycling.

1. Draw a mind map to plan your summary. Use headings and key words to summarise the main points in the report.
2. Each choose one section of the report and write a summary of one paragraph in your own words. Write a section heading and begin with a topic sentence.

> **Tip**
> Use a range of complex sentences and correct punctuation!

3. Put your paragraphs together under one main heading. Add illustrations.
4. Display your work.

B Compare summaries.

Discuss the following points:
- For each summary, is the information divided into sections with headings?
- Are the sections placed in the same order in all the summaries?
- Do all the summaries sound the same?

Unit 8 Make it happen

10 and 11 Write a non-chronological report

A Write a report for your school principal on the topic of recycling in your school. Make recommendations in your report to start a recycling campaign. If your school already has a recycling programme, your report should be an update on how the programme is doing and how it could expand.

1 To begin, gather information, facts and statistics that will help you write the report. Here are some ideas:

- Keep a 'waste journal' for a week. Each day record your observations about how much waste and what waste is generated.
- Conduct interviews with pupils and teachers. Find out what people do with their rubbish.
- Carry out a survey to find out if anything is needed to help people to recycle.

2 Once you have collected information and data, plan your report in sections.

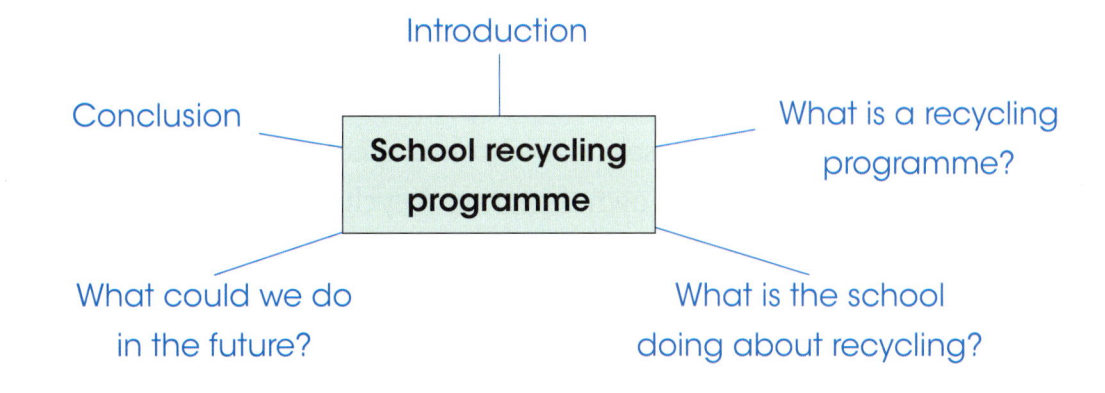

- Introduction
- Conclusion
- What is a recycling programme?
- What could we do in the future?
- What is the school doing about recycling?

(Central topic: **School recycling programme**)

3 Write a first draft. Include facts and some opinions and a picture or diagram e.g. a graph to show the results of some of your research.

4 Ask a talk partner to proofread your report and suggest improvements. Edit your work carefully and write out your final work neatly.

> **Tip**
>
> Remember to include the important language features that will help to improve your writing:
> - conditional clauses
> - complex sentences with a range of connectives
> - a formal style using the third person
> - correct punctuation
> - good vocabulary.

12 Create a group magazine

A Compile a group magazine.

1 In groups, review the written work you've done in this unit and choose one piece of work each for the magazine.

2 Work together to make a front cover, a contents page and a back page with a list of the contributors.

> **Tip**
>
> Look through some real magazines to see how to lay the pages out.

B Pass your finished magazines around the class to read, and then deliver them to another class for them to enjoy!

> **How did I do?**
> - Did I read and summarise a non-chronological report?
> - Did I plan and write my own report on recycling?
> - Did I compile a magazine with my group?

9 Snapshot

Poems can create a 'snapshot' of a meaningful moment or memory. In this unit you'll read about tropical fruit, an African antelope and cutting a pomegranate, and you'll peel back layers of meaning beneath the skin of the poems.

Vocabulary to learn and use: pomegranate, jasmine, myrtle, garnet, lustrous, impala, acacia, copse, astringency, sapodilla, pawpaw

1 Fruit in a bowl

A Poems can teach us to see something ordinary with fresh eyes.

1 **a** What sort of fruit do you eat? Is it local or **exotic**?
   b Describe your favourite fruit to a group – its look, colour, smell and taste. Use similes.

2 Read the poem *Fruit in a Bowl* by Guyanese poet A.J. Seymour. First skim over it to get a feel for it; then read it aloud with a talk partner.

exotic *adj.* unusual, interesting and often foreign

Fruit in a Bowl

Fruit in a bowl.

Full goldenapples with veined skins so fine
That just a look might burst them –

    tangerines
For all the world like small green solid bells
Promising little kisses of **astringency**.

Yellow bananas, cool and firm to feel
Lying in curves of silken-tongued delight.

Caribbean goldenapple

Green tangerines

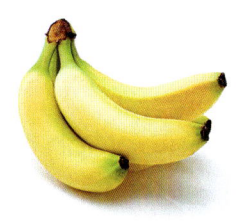

Bananas

Mangoes

Session 1 Fruit in a bowl 145

And great plumpted mangoes, sweetness to the seed.
Huge cut pawpaws bearing dark-seedling cargoes.

And sapodillas with their sweet, brown kernels
Aching to change to sugar once again.

Tropical fruit.

A.J. Seymour

Pawpaw   Sapodillas

> **astringency** *n.* sharpness of taste that makes the mouth pucker
> **tropical** *adj.* in or from the hottest parts of the world

3 Tell each other your initial impressions of the poem.

Did you know?

Guyana is in the Caribbean. Its official name is the Cooperative Republic of Guyana. The Caribbean has lots of palm trees and tropical fruit.

B Poems don't always have an exact meaning. Talking about poems helps us to appreciate them through each other's eyes.

1 Do you think the poem is written in the poet's voice or in a narrator's voice? Why do you think so?

2 a How many of the fruits do you know? Have you tasted any?
  b What fruits from your region would you choose for a poem?

3 What format or pattern is used to describe each fruit?

4 Sketch your impression of the bowl of fruit based on the poem.

C The poem describes tropical fruit in a bowl, but is it more than that?

1 Why do you think the poet might have chosen to write a poem about fruit in a bowl?

2 What else might he be thinking about? What might the fruit bowl remind him of?

3 Write a short paragraph about the poem in a group.
  a Start with a topic sentence to say what the poem is about.
  b Include your favourite image in the poem.

c Explain how the poet uses something ordinary to describe something important to him.

d Conclude your paragraph with an idea for something you would choose to create a snapshot or memory of your 'home'.

2 Poetic form and features

A Poems come in many forms; some have no obvious form at all.

1 Re-read *Fruit in a Bowl* with a talk partner. Describe the form to each other. Take turns to mention features and give examples.

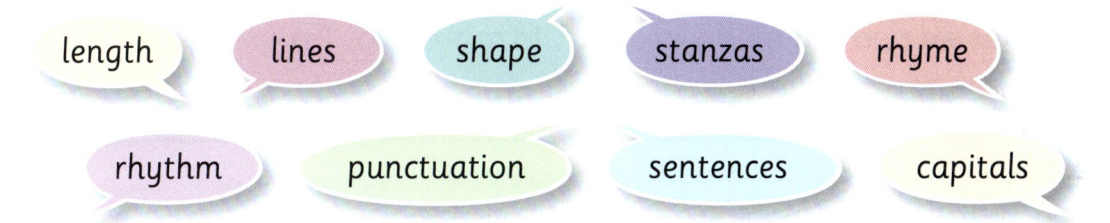

> length   lines   shape   stanzas   rhyme
>
> rhythm   punctuation   sentences   capitals

2 Which adjectives describe the language style?

> flowery   complicated   simple   stark   precise
> dull   unpretentious   fancy   plain   conversational

3 Predict the meaning of any unfamiliar words using the context. Does the dictionary agree?

4 a Which adjective would not appear in the dictionary?
  b What does it describe about the fruit?
  c Why do you think the poet used an invented word?

5 a Are the fruit descriptions literal, figurative or both? Why?
  b Which poetic devices does the poet use?

> similes   metaphors   personification
> alliteration   onomatopoeia   assonance

B Read the poem closely to answer these questions.

1 How does the layout of the lines give the idea of fruit in a bowl?
2 Describe the contrasts in the flow of lines in the poem.
3 The poem has no complete sentences. How does this match the way the poet lists the different fruits?

C In a group, add three more fruits to *Fruit in a Bowl*.

1 **a** Suggest one fruit each. Tell each other how your fruit looks, tastes, smells and feels. Which details encapsulate your fruit?
  b Find precise words in a thesaurus to create your image. Include some figurative language.
  c Include an invented word for your fruit – like *plumpted*.

> **encapsulate** *v.*
> express or show the most important facts about something

Language focus

Prefixes give clues about meanings of words.
The prefixes **en** and **em** mean 'in', 'into', 'to make into'. For example:
encapsulate, encourage, enrich, entrust, empower, enrage, enclose.

2 Review your group's fruits and suggest improvements, thinking about the choice of words and images. Read the new lines aloud to check for flow.
3 Add your fruits anywhere in the poem, where they fit. Then share your poem with the class.

> **Any volunteers?**
> *Capsula* is the Latin word for a capsule – a small container! Can you see how the word *encapsulate* has been formed?

3 There for a moment

A Do you know what an impala is?

Impala

Medium-sized antelope, 75–95 cm high, weighing 40–60 kg. Found in southern parts of Africa in savannahs and thicker bush-land. Grazes on fresh grass and foliage. Males (rams) have curved horns up to 90 cm in length. Females (ewes) have no horns.

1. What information does the fact file give?
2. Skim over the next poem, *Impala*, on page 150. Read it with a talk partner; first agree who will read each part.
3. Take turns to read the poem again as your partner listens with closed eyes, imagining the scene. Don't rush your reading – take your time in between each stanza.

B Discuss *Impala*.

1. Tell each other the story in the poem. Which part is your favourite?
2. Why do you think the poet wrote about this scene? What do you think inspires him?
3. What inspires you? What moment or object could you write about to celebrate it?

C The poem captures a small scene that represents something much greater: the beauty of nature in the African bush.

1. Have a discussion forum. Use examples from the poem.
   a. Do you think the poet has ever done or seen what he describes?
   b. Did the poem or the fact file tell you more about the impala?
   c. Choose a word or phrase to describe the theme of this poem.
   d. Did you enjoy the poem? Why? How did it make you feel?
   e. Present your group's ideas in an interesting or unusual way on a large piece of card. Be creative!

Impala

Imagine, for a moment,
As you lift your eyes
<u>from the panting plains</u>
to the gentle rise where
a shady **copse** of **Acacia**
trees
has green young leaf buds
cooled by the breeze
that you see
with the sight
of a hunter.

Look

a leafless branch curves
just enough
to be a horn
dark-ridged and rough
    the rich red browns
you took for ground are rippling shoulders
sleek and
round above the flanks-pale fawn –
the colours of a drying thorn

Impala!

<u>Suddenly swift when put to flight</u>
<u>the impala leaps and</u>
<u>soars in fright then streams away across</u>
<u>the plains</u>

   <u>and stands</u>

     <u>to watch the danger past.</u>
                Ted Townsend

> **copse** *n.* a small group of trees
> **acacia** *n.* a tree from warm parts of the world that has small leaves and yellow or white flowers

4 Features for effect

Tip

I am = first person
you are = second person
he, she, it is = third person

A 📖 💬 📝 Re-read the poem *Impala* closely in pairs before answering in your notebook.

1. Is the poem told in first, second or third person? How can you tell?
2. Whose voice is it – the narrator's or the poet's? How can you tell?
3. What tense is the poem written in? Give examples.
4. What effect do the tense and the narrative voice help to achieve?
5. What does *Imagine … that you see with the sight of a hunter* mean? Is this a literal or a figurative expression?
6. Rephrase the underlined words from the poem in your own words.
7. What figures of speech or poetic devices are used in each one?

Tip

Figurative language creates an effect beyond the literal meaning of the words: similes, metaphors, personification, alliteration, onomatopoeia.

8. **a** Choose an adjective to describe the style and mood of the poem.

   conversational   formal   stilted
   reflective   relaxed   tense   mysterious

   b How do the lines running on into each other help create this feel?
   c What is the effect of the single lines in between the stanzas and at the end?
   d Is the feel and pace of the poem similar all the way through?

Tip

Poets often use non-Standard English or unusual punctuation and layout for effect – it's poetic licence!

9. **a** Why do you think the poem has so little punctuation?
   b What is the effect of having so little punctuation?
   c Which punctuation mark is used for dramatic effect in the poem? Explain the effect.

Did you know?

If a thought or idea finishes at the end of a line with a full stop, this is called an *end-stopped line*.

If a thought spills over from one line into the next without a punctuated pause at the end of the line, it's called *enjambment*.

B Compare the poetic features of *Fruit in a Bowl* and *Impala*.

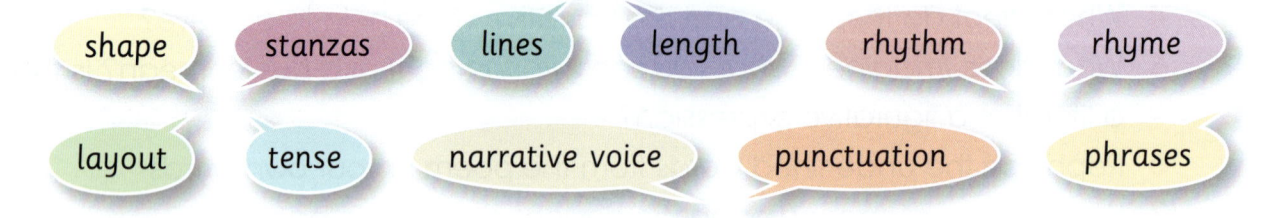

- shape
- stanzas
- lines
- length
- rhythm
- rhyme
- layout
- tense
- narrative voice
- punctuation
- phrases

1 Compare the features of the poems. Use an organising tool such as a table or a mind map to organise your notes.

Features	A Bowl of Fruit	Impala	Comment
stanzas	7 stanzas	3 main stanzas	Both have short, uneven lines
rhyme	No rhyme		
tense			

5 A jewel

A Memories are a great source of inspiration for poems. Flashbacks can be very powerful – scenes are remembered in vivid detail, which over time come to mean more than the original moment.

1 a Have you eaten a pomegranate? Do you know how it looks and tastes?
  b Read the pomegranate fact file. Does it make you want to try one?

Pomegranate (*Punica granatum*)

Native to North Africa and western Asia; a fruit-bearing, deciduous shrub or small tree growing 5–8 metres tall. The tree bears a spherical fruit with a tough golden-orange outer skin with sweet, red, gelatinous flesh with seeds.

2 Skim over *How to Cut a Pomegranate* by Imtiaz Dharker on page 154 to get a feel for it. Then read the poem aloud in pairs, one reading the narrative, one reading the father's words.

Imtiaz Dharker, poet, artist and film-maker, was born in Pakistan. She was brought up in Scotland and now lives in India, England and Wales. She writes about home, freedom, journeys and **displacement**.

> **displacement** *n.* when people have to leave where they normally live

B **The poem draws the reader in to share the snapshot.**
1. What story features does the poem have?
2. How do the long and short sentences, enjambment and end-stopped lines mirror the father's actions?
3. How does the poet create the conversational feel?

C Did you notice that most of the poem was a flashback? Add the poem to your learning journal; include examples of its poetic techniques. Say whether you enjoyed the poem.

How to Cut a Pomegranate

'Never,' said my father.
'Never cut a pomegranate
through the heart. It will weep blood.
Treat it delicately, with respect.

Just slit the upper skin across four quarters.
This is a magic fruit,
so when you split it open, be prepared
for the jewels of the world to tumble out,
more precious than garnets,
more lustrous than rubies,
lit as if from inside.
Each jewel contains a living seed.
Separate one crystal.
Hold it up to catch the light.
Inside is a whole universe.
No common jewel can give you this.'

Afterwards, I tried to make necklaces
of pomegranate seeds.
The juice spurted out, bright crimson,
and stained my fingers, then my mouth.

I didn't mind. The juice tasted of gardens
I had never seen, **voluptuous**
with myrtle, lemon, jasmine,
and alive with parrots' wings.

The pomegranate reminded me
that somewhere I had another home.

Imtiaz Dharker

voluptuous *adj.* luscious and appealing to the senses

6 Try 'encapsulating' a snapshot

A In *How to Cut a Pomegranate*, the poet describes something ordinary and makes it extraordinary through vivid description, detail and a comparison with something precious.

> You could tell your father or mother how to eat something special – or a younger brother or sister, or even a friend.

1. Choose something you particularly like to eat as inspiration for your poem *How to eat a … .*
2. Plan your poem using a mind map. Follow the form of the pomegranate poem. Start with a strong word like *never* or *always*, or a strong verb or a command like *cut, slice, open* or *peel*.

Which food?

Stanza 1
Strong start
It's a conversation with …
What to do/not to do literally

Stanza 2
Develop the comparison
Use figurative language,
short and long
sentences, enjambment

Stanzas 3–4
Describe what you like
about eating it
What it makes you smell,
taste, see

Stanza 5
End with a reflection – what
does your food remind you of?

3. Write a first draft. Ask a talk partner to suggest improvements.
   - Focus on the style and images.
   - Proofread carefully, especially the dialogue punctuation.
4. Display your poem in neat, joined-up handwriting.
   - Add imaginative drawings or online images.
   - Include a brief, factual fact file on your food.

How did I do?

- Did I plan a poem using a mind map?
- Did I include correctly punctuated dialogue, illustrations and a fact file?
- Did I work with my talk partner to revise and improve my poem?

Term 1 Spelling activities

A   Revise common spelling sounds

The vowels (a, e, i, o, u) all have a long and a short sound: *mat – mate*; *pet – Pete*; *bit – bite*; *not – note*; *cut – cute*. The long vowel sounds can be made by various letter patterns.

1 **a** Discuss the letter patterns that make the long 'a' sound in these words:

> flake   day   main   rein   they   eight   agent

   b Find another word for each of the letter patterns with the same sound.

2 **a** Which of these words contain the long 'a' sound?

> fete   match   gauge   autumn   straight
> panic   real   pass   aunt   crochet

   b Use each one in a sentence. Use a dictionary to check meanings.

B   Recognising unstressed syllables

Each syllable of a word has one vowel sound, as in *hat, sit, not, neat, bait, fly* and *close*. In words with more than one syllable, we don't stress each syllable equally but they are still important for spelling.

1 Say these two-syllable words aloud. Did you stress the underlined or the non-underlined syllable?

> <u>moun</u>tain   <u>drag</u>on   <u>Min</u>li   <u>riv</u>er   <u>vill</u>age   <u>fruit</u>ful   <u>fruit</u>less

2 Say these three-syllable words aloud. Which syllable did you stress the most? Which the least?

> butterfly   triangle   umbrella   alphabet   computer   introduce

3 Which vowel sound is not pronounced clearly (unstressed) in these words?

> chocolate   library   interesting   business   medicine   family
> separate   jewellery   vegetable   miniature   history   diamond

> **Tip**
>
> To remember how to spell words with unstressed vowels, stress each vowel sound equally – like *mys-ter-y*. It will help you hear all the vowel sounds.

C AZ Prefixes can give clues to meanings

1 Work out the meaning of the underlined prefixes.
   a <u>mid</u>day   <u>mid</u>night   <u>mid</u>week   <u>mid</u>winter   <u>mid</u>summer
   b <u>re</u>write   <u>re</u>place   <u>re</u>mind   <u>re</u>do   <u>re</u>turn
   c <u>multi</u>cultural   <u>multi</u>millionaire   <u>multi</u>lingual   <u>multi</u>ply
2 Discuss each root word and how the prefix changes its meaning.
3 Write sentences demonstrating the meaning of two words from each group.

D AZ Suffixes can change the meaning of words

The suffix *ful* means 'full of'. The suffix *less* means 'without'.

1 Copy this table into your notebook and complete it with each of these root words.

   hope   colour   thought   harm   power   help   taste

Add suffix –less	Root word	Add suffix ful
careless	care	careful

2 a What is the word class of these words?

   beautiful   penniless   plentiful   merciless   bountiful   fanciful

   b What root word is each word formed from?
   c What word class does each root word belong to?
   d Using your prior knowledge, discuss the rule used to spell the words in the box above.

> **Tip**
>
> Remember that although the suffix *ful* means 'full of', it is spelled with one *l*.

E Tricky endings

Some adjectives' endings sound very similar, like *ible* and *able*. The suffix *ible* is used for words with a Latin origin; *able* came originally from French and is used for words that do not have Latin roots.

Latin origin

audible divisible visible possible legible responsible flexible edible

French origin

manageable capable fashionable comfortable
acceptable enjoyable workable readable eatable

1. Write the words in joined-up writing in your notebook to remember their feel.
2. Next to each word, write its antonym by adding a prefix (*in im ir il* or *un*).
3. Practise using the words and their antonyms in sentences.
4. Work with a talk partner to think of more *ible* and *able* words and add them to your lists.

F Not wrong, just different

Words are not all spelled the same way everywhere. How are these words spelled in your region?

1. Can you spot any letter patterns that change between UK and US spellings?
2. Form a rule out of any letter patterns you notice more than once.

UK English spelling	US English spelling	UK English spelling	US English spelling
grey	gray	neighbour	neighbor
centre	center	gaol	jail
colour	color	favour	favor
cancelled	canceled	dialled	dialed
kilometre	kilometer	axe	ax
mould	mold	centimetre	centimeter

Term 2 Spelling activities

A Revise common spelling sounds

The letter *c* is found in various letter patterns which make different sounds: 'k', 's', 'ch' or 'sh'.

1. Draw up four lists in your notebook, one for each sound.
   a. Sort the words in the box under the four headings, according to the sound the letter *c* is part of.
   b. In each list underline the letter or letters that make the sound.
   c. Add as many words as you can to each list.
   d. Discuss the ways each sound is made up.

> kind   comb   ocean   cattle   scene   luck   city   equator   acclaim
> bicycle   chat   occupy   school   match   folk   science   chunk   chemist
> brochure   back   stomach   yolk   kitten   chalk   acquire   antique
> machine   conquer   chorus   cent   racquet   thatch   bucket

2. a. In pairs or groups, think of as many words as you can with the long 'o' sound (as in *bone*). Sort your words according to the letter patterns that make the 'o' sound.
   b. Share your lists with another pair or group and discuss any differences.

B Soft and hard *c* and *g*

When *c* and *g* are followed by the vowels *a*, *o* or *u*, they have a hard sound. When they are followed by the vowels *i* and *e*, they have a soft sound ('s' and 'j').

1. Say the following words and write them in your notebook under four lists with the headings *Soft c*, *Hard c*, *Soft g* and *Hard g*.

> gem   crisp   agile   clasp   census   age   logical
> dialogue   wedge   brave   garden   citizen   cell

2. Devise a way to remember these exceptions: *get, girl, gear, give, tiger*.
3. You could use these ideas on page 160.

Think of other words it's like. Listen to the sound and see the letter pattern.
get – bet, let, met

Write a mnemonic.
Gold Elephants Talk!

Write it in joined-up handwriting to fix the feel of the word. get, get, get

You can use these techniques to remember any difficult spellings!

C AZ Forming nouns from verbs

1 Identify the root verb and suffix used to create these nouns.

> payment   treatment   agreement   replacement
> entertainment   government   arrangement

Tip

Watch out for the *n* in *government* – it is not sounded out very clearly.

2 Write sentences to demonstrate the meaning of each noun. Read them out to a talk partner leaving a blank for the word. Let your partner guess which one to use.

3 Some nouns are the same as the related verb, for example *talk*. Can you think of any others?

4 Use these words in sentences to show which is the noun and which is the verb.

> sing/song   think/thought   practise/practice   build/building   jog/jogger

Term 2 Spelling activities

D Working with opposite prefixes

Some prefixes make words mean the opposite: *un, dis, in, im, ir, il, non, anti*.

1 Discuss which prefix to use for each word in the box.

> **Tip**
> Remembering how words sound can be really helpful for spelling. Try saying the root word with each prefix and listen for which one sounds right.

> correct   regular   fair   agree   legible   clockwise   possible
> honest   successful   polite   responsible   legal   official
> formal   even   reversible   perfect   social

2 Devise a rule or a reminder to help you remember tricky ones like *in, im, ir* and *il*.

> **Did you know?**
> The prefix *anti* comes from ancient Greek; *non, dis, in, im, ir* and *il* all come from Latin. Only *un* is of English origin.

E Revise a spelling rule

If a word ends in a short vowel followed by a single consonant, double the last consonant when adding a suffix that begins with a vowel (*ing, ed, er/ar/or*; e.g. *beg* → *begged, begging, beggar*).

> **Tip**
> Words with one syllable also count as the last syllable!

1 Which of these words would double the last syllable if followed by *ing*?

> rebel   join   stand   repeat   flap   run   walk   admit   tip   stay   begin   regret

2 Write the past participle (*ed*) of these words in your notebook.

> spot   flake   stay   refer   use   step   pat   equal   commit   grab   slip

  a What did you do about the verbs ending in silent *e*?
  b What are the root verbs from these participles: *snowed, gazed, faxed*?
  c What does this tell you about exceptions to the rule?

Term 2 Spelling activities

Term 3 Spelling activities

A Revise common spelling sounds

1   a   Read aloud the words in the box to find those that contain a 'j' sound.
    b   Sort the words into lists by letter pattern. Underline the letters that make the 'j' sound.

    dge – he<u>dge</u> / dj – a<u>dj</u>ust / ge – privile<u>ge</u> / j – <u>j</u>am / gi – <u>gi</u>gantic / gy – apolo<u>gy</u>

    c   Put each list into alphabetical order.
    d   Find small words inside your lists to help you remember the spelling.

> cage   adjust   gigantic   adjective   soldier   gate   manage
> apology   encourage   trudge   siege   gorge   hedge   refuge
> wedge   grudge   gymnast   object   gadget   got   fidget   gale
> wedge   adjourn   bridge   genius   gloat   mango   stranger
> glamorous   foliage   heritage   jam   jealous   job   challenge
> ginger   village   giraffe   adjacent   smudge   privilege   injure

2   Think of as many words with the sound 'er' as you can and add them to a mind map of your own, sorted by letter pattern.

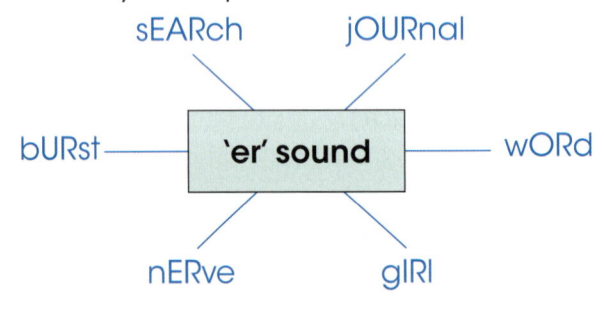

```
             sEARch      jOURnal
                  \      /
                   \    /
     bURst ——— 'er' sound ——— wORd
                   /    \
                  /      \
               nERve     gIRl
```

B Choose precise words

Synonyms in a thesaurus may not have exactly the same meaning. For example, *throw, toss, chuck, fling, lob* and *pitch* all have slightly different shades of meaning.

1   Replace the underlined words with different synonyms. How does each synonym change the meaning of the sentence?

   Gisela <u>looked</u> at her brother. (stared, observed, glanced, watched, gazed)

   a   The parents <u>complained</u> about the noise.
   b   The children <u>ran</u> through the field.
   c   The animal <u>ate</u> the food.

2 Choose a synonym to change the effect of the sentence.
   a The boy wrote a letter.
   b Ayanda smiled at her classmate.
   c The bird flew over the school each morning.

C AZ Homophones and homographs

> **Language focus**
>
> Homophones **sound the same** but are spelled differently.
> Homographs are **spelled the same** but may have a different sound.
> Homograph and homophone pairs or groups of words have **different meanings**.

1 a Find pairs or groups of **homophones** in the box below. Write them in your notebook. Check you know their meanings.
   b Write sentences for **three** sets of homophones to demonstrate their meanings.

> guest idol sent poor idle flaw allowed vein threw
> pour site cent through weather rode knead son
> aloud vain need whether muscle scent shore their
> too road they're pore to kneed guessed rowed two
> sure won floor sun paw vane sight one there mussel

2 a Use a dictionary to identify the word classes of the **homographs** in the following box.
   b Create sentences to show the different meanings of these homographs.

> bow fair content down object refuse wind
> second tear wound wave bat lead

row
1 noun – I sit in the back row of the cinema.
2 noun – The neighbours had a row about who should trim the hedge.
3 verb – I had to row the boat across the river because the engine broke down.

D AZ The prefix *ad*

The prefix *ad* comes from Latin and means 'to' or 'in the direction of'.

When *ad* is added to a word beginning with *c, f, g, l, n, p, r, s* or *t*, the *d* usually changes to match the first letter of the word (e.g. *ad* + *cept* = *accept*; *ad* + *fix* = *affix*; *ad* + *sure* = *assure*).

If the word begins with *d*, *ad* remains the same (e.g. *ad* + *dress* = *address*).

If the word begins with a vowel, the *d* is not doubled (e.g. *ad* + *apt* = *adapt*; *ad* + *ore* = *adore*).

1 How many words can you find that follow this pattern? Work with a talk partner.
   a Use a dictionary to find and list words with a double consonant after the *ad/a*.
   b Make a second list of words without a double consonant after *ad*.
   c Test each other on the spellings.

> **Tip**
> Write the words in joined-up handwriting to fix the feel of the word. Practise using the LOOK SAY COVER WRITE CHECK technique.

E AZ Revise a spelling rule

When a word ends in a consonant + *e*, drop the *e* when adding a suffix that begins with a vowel (*ing, ed, er/ar/or*; e.g. *create* → *creating*).

Write the rule in your learning journal with these verbs and any others you meet to remind you to drop the *e*.

arrive   breathe   dazzle   excuse   investigate
oppose   promise   rejoice   sparkle   wriggle

Toolkit

Presentation skills

Presentation and final work should always be in your best joined-up handwriting or typed up using ICT – for example, a Word processor.

Handwriting

Apart from looking good, joined-up handwriting helps you fix the feel of words in your head and your hand, which improves your spelling too. Concentrate on:
- writing exactly on the lines
- evenly spaced letters inside words and evenly spaced words in sentences
- tall letters all the same height (except for *t* which is a bit shorter)
- small letters the same height and on a level with the bottom part of *b*, *d*, *h* and *k*
- letters finishing below the line in the right place
- capitals all the same height and as tall as your tall letters.

If you use blank paper, always use guidelines behind the paper to keep the lines straight with a margin.

Tips to make your writing stand out and be easy to read

- Underline headings neatly or use a coloured pen for display work.
- Cut out your writing neatly and mount it on coloured card or paper.
- Draw a neat black or coloured border using a ruler.

Computers

If you use acomputer to write out your work, remember to:
- use the spell check feature at the end to check your spelling and grammar
- use a medium font size and sensible line spacing – not too big, not too small
- choose a font that will be easy to read as well as nice to look at
- insert any pictures or diagrams carefully so that the text is still easy to read
- use bold, colours and larger font sizes for headings – but don't have too many styles in your work.

Nuts and bolts of writing

Sentences, paragraphs and connectives

Sentences are groups of words that give information or say something. They are the building blocks of good writing, both fiction and non-fiction. If you understand how sentences work, you can then work with them to extend them, join them or link them to add meaning and variety to your writing.

Basic sentence rules

Sentences begin with a capital letter and end with a full stop, exclamation mark or question mark. A sentence contains a verb and must make sense.

There are three types of sentence:

- statements – used to state facts
- questions – used to ask questions
- commands – used to give orders or instructions.

Types of sentences and connectives

Simple sentences say one thing – although they can be very detailed if extended with descriptive phrases.

Compound sentences are two main clauses joined by a coordinating conjunction or a connective. Each part of the sentence would make sense on its own. They are usually joined to add flow and variety.

Coordinating conjunctions connect words, phrases and clauses: *for, and, nor, but, or, yet, so* (FANBOYS).

Complex sentences have one main clause and one or more dependent clauses. They are dependent because they would not make sense without the main clause. They are linked to the main clause by subordinating conjunctions or connectives; they are often known as subordinate clauses.

Subordinating conjunctions or connectives have a clear purpose in a sentence. Common subordinating connectives: *if, while, although, because, therefore, in addition, for example.*

Connectives can also link paragraphs and sentences to show how they are connected to each other, for example in a time sequence.

Purpose	Connective
Addition	further, and, in addition, additionally, also
Consequence	as a result, thus, therefore
Contrast	but, however, yet, on the other hand
Comparison	similarly, equally, while
Purpose	so that, in order that
Concession	although, granted, yet
Time	meanwhile, before that, after that, since then
Sequence	then, next, finally, first, second, third
Condition	if, then, provided, as long as, whether
Reason	because, since, so
Example	for example, such as, for instance, in particular
Conclusion	finally, in conclusion, thus, therefore

Structure of a non-fiction paragraph

A good paragraph in non-fiction writing has a clear topic sentence (usually the first sentence) to say what the paragraph is about. The next sentences give the detail relating to the paragraph topic. The final sentence concludes the paragraph or leads on to the next paragraph topic.

> Cape Town is the second largest city in South Africa. It is situated between Table Mountain and the coast with its many beaches. The Atlantic Ocean is on one side of the city but on the other it is the Indian Ocean. Cape Town has a large harbour with many cruise ships docking to see the sights in and around the Cape Town area, so tourism is an important industry. Many people believe Cape Town is one of the most beautiful cities in the world.

Starting a new paragraph

Writers start a new paragraph to signpost a new idea, a different topic, a change in direction or a change of scene. In fiction a new paragraph is started each time a new person speaks. Paragraphs are often linked by connectives, adverbs or adverbial phrases (e.g. *After cooking breakfast …; The next day …; Finally …*

Toolkit

Keeping a learning journal

A learning journal is a good place to remember useful techniques, practise your own skills and record what you do and don't like. You can even include clips and cut-outs from magazines, advertisements or visual images that inspire you.

Use your journal to keep a record of your reading – the different genres, extracts or whole books, fiction or non-fiction.

You can also include your personal responses to texts, including:

- a review of books read, together with recommendations for others to read the book
- your reactions to characters and events
- predictions and questions about the plot
- summaries of the plot development in each chapter
- reflective writing in the role of one of the characters (e.g. a diary)
- examples of successful or evocative sentences
- examples of unfamiliar and archaic language use, or words borrowed from other languages
- examples of other language use (e.g. colloquial, conversational or formal language), including idioms and proverbs you have come across and would like to remember
- quotations or extracts from texts to use as models
- vocabulary you would like to use again.

You can stick in pictures, headlines and articles you have cut out from newspapers and magazines, or examples of writing in different media such as advertisements, recipes, instructions, leaflets and brochures. You might even find some reviews of books you have read or would like to read. You can also keep a personal list of favourite new words at the back to use in your own writing.

Be as creative as you like!

Using an etymological dictionary

Etymological dictionaries give you information about a word's origin – the language the word comes from. They can be confusing compared with an everyday dictionary.

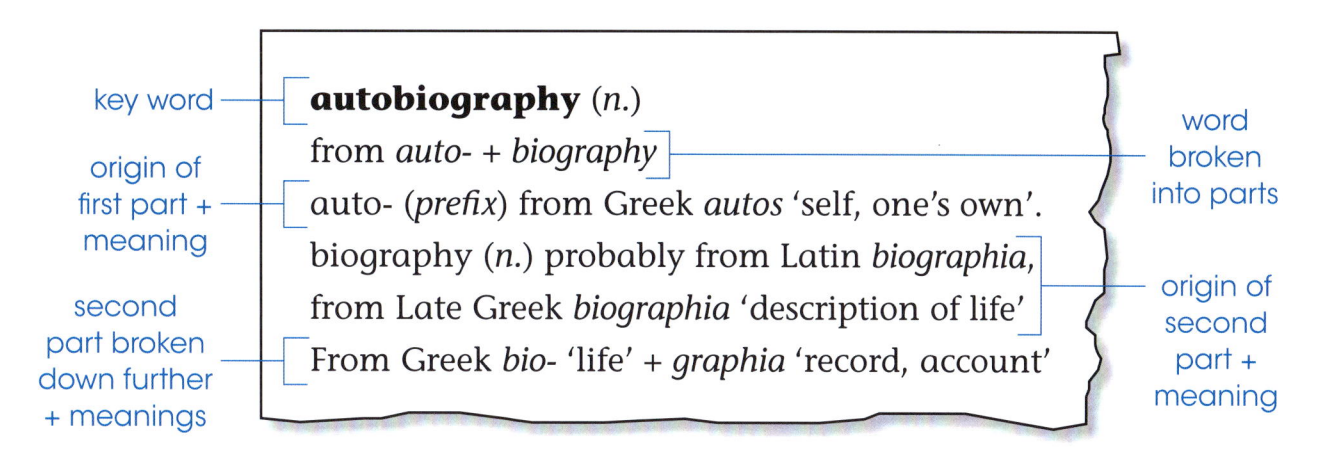

- key word → **autobiography** (*n.*)
- word broken into parts → from *auto-* + *biography*
- origin of first part + meaning → *auto-* (*prefix*) from Greek *autos* 'self, one's own'.
- *biography* (*n.*) probably from Latin *biographia*, from Late Greek *biographia* 'description of life'
- origin of second part + meaning
- second part broken down further + meanings → From Greek *bio-* 'life' + *graphia* 'record, account'

Unit 1: Listening text

Learner book page 23 & 24

Oliver Strange and the Journey to the Swamps by Dianne Hofmeyr

Oliver has flown to Africa to find his scientist father. The minute he lands in Bulawayo in Zimbabwe, nothing goes according to plan. Before he knows it, he is on a bus to Victoria Falls with a girl called Zinzi and a bushbaby called Bobo. This extract is the end of Chapter 4 and the beginning of Chapter 5.

Toolkit 169

He turned away from Zinzi. *He* wasn't the one who was weird. *This* was what was weird:

1. His aunt hadn't been in Bulawayo to meet him.
2. He was travelling with a python.
3. A creepy, sinister man was following him.
4. Ilalaland wasn't a place after all.
5. The plans he'd made with Grandma in Tooting had gone upside down.
6. Tooting was far away … a zillion, million miles away. Another life.
7. And worse than everything, he wasn't any closer to finding his father than before. Now his father had *truly* disappeared.

Chapter 5 Tooting, London – Wanted Alive

The whole episode started three weeks before when he'd stared down at the globe on the kitchen table in Tooting.

"He's gone, Grandma!"

"Who?"

"Dad! He's completely and utterly disappeared."

His grandmother looked up from her sudoku puzzle in *The Times*. 'What do you mean, utterly disappeared?'

"He's gone. It happens, Grandma. People disappear."

"Objects disappear, Oliver. *People* don't!"

"Yes, they do!"

"Not people like your father. It would be hard to make him disappear."

Ollie spun the globe. The colours blurred under his hand. The pattern of red dots snaked like an intricate belt around the earth's middle. Each dot was a red sticker that he'd stuck to the globe to mark a place his father had been to.

The stickers encircled the world. There was no beginning and no end to them.

The red snake began in South China. Then it wriggled its way through Vietnam, Cambodia and Thailand, then stretched across to Madagascar, and coiled up through Mozambique, Tanzania and over the Congo, across the ocean through the Amazon to Peru and ended up by catching its own tail as it slithered its way through the islands of the Pacific Ocean.

His father had travelled just about everywhere in the world.

All in the quest for frogs.

Why? Why was he so *obsessed* with frogs?

Unit 2: Biography

Amelia Earhart – a timeline

1897 (24th July)	Born in a small town in Kansas, USA
1921	Learned to fly
	Bought her first plane – bright yellow biplane, 'The Canary'
1922	Achieved world altitude record for women pilots, 14 000 feet (4267 metres)
1928	Crossed the Atlantic as part of a crew of three
	Published first book, *20 Hrs. 40 Min.*, about transatlantic flight
1932	Flew a plane solo across Atlantic Ocean
1937 (2nd July)	Went missing in a plane over Pacific Ocean
	Her book *Last Flight* about her planned flight around the world published by her husband
2012	Search for wreckage uncovers more clues about mystery of her death

Unit 3: Poems

Here are the full versions of the poems.

- The Brook – page 47
- The Cataract of Lodore – page 54

The Brook

I come from haunts of coot and hern,
I make a sudden sally
And sparkle out among the fern,
To bicker down a valley.

By thirty hills I hurry down,
Or slip between the ridges,
By twenty thorpes, a little town,
And half a hundred bridges.

Till last by Philip's farm I flow
To join the brimming river,
For men may come and men may go,
But I go on for ever.

I chatter over stony ways,
In little sharps and trebles,
I bubble into eddying bays,
I babble on the pebbles.

With many a curve my banks I fret
By many a field and fallow,
And many a fairy foreland set
With willow-weed and mallow.

I chatter, chatter, as I flow
To join the brimming river,
For men may come and men may go,
But I go on for ever.

I wind about, and in and out,
With here a blossom sailing,
And here and there a lusty trout,
And here and there a grayling,

And here and there a foamy flake
Upon me, as I travel
With many a silvery waterbreak
Above the golden gravel,

And draw them all along, and flow
To join the brimming river
For men may come and men may go,
But I go on for ever.

I steal by lawns and grassy plots,
I slide by hazel covers;
I move the sweet forget-me-nots
That grow for happy lovers.

I slip, I slide, I gloom, I glance,
Among my skimming swallows;
I make the netted sunbeam dance
Against my sandy shallows.

I murmur under moon and stars
In brambly wildernesses;
I linger by my shingly bars;
I loiter round my cresses;

And out again I curve and flow
To join the brimming river,
For men may come and men may go,
But I go on for ever.

Alfred Lord Tennyson

The Cataract of Lodore

"How does the water
Come down at Lodore?"
My little boy asked me
Thus, once on a time;
And moreover he tasked me
To tell him in rhyme.
Anon, at the word,
There first came one daughter,
And then came another,
To second and third
The request of their brother,
And to hear how the water
Comes down at Lodore,
With its rush and its roar,
As many a time
They had seen it before.
So I told them in rhyme,
For of rhymes I had store;
And 'twas in my vocation
For their recreation
That so I should sing;
Because I was Laureate
To them and the King.

From its sources which well
In the tarn on the fell;
From its fountains
In the mountains,
Its rills and its gills;
Through moss and through brake,
It runs and it creeps
For a while, till it sleeps
In its own little lake.
And thence at departing,
Awakening and starting,

It runs through the reeds,
And away it proceeds,
Through meadow and glade,
In sun and in shade,
And through the wood-shelter,
Among crags in its flurry,
Helter-skelter,
Hurry-skurry.
Here it comes sparkling,
And there it lies darkling;
Now smoking and frothing
Its tumult and wrath in,
Till, in this rapid race
On which it is bent,
It reaches the place
Of its steep descent.

The cataract strong
Then plunges along,
Striking and raging
As if a war waging
Its caverns and rocks among;
Rising and leaping,
Sinking and creeping,
Swelling and sweeping,
Showering and springing,
Flying and flinging,
Writhing and ringing,
Eddying and whisking,
Spouting and frisking,
Turning and twisting,
Around and around
With endless rebound:
Smiting and fighting,
A sight to delight in;

Confounding, astounding,
Dizzying and deafening the ear with its sound.

Collecting, projecting,
Receding and speeding,
And shocking and rocking,
And darting and parting,
And threading and spreading,
And whizzing and hissing,
And dripping and skipping,
And hitting and splitting,
And shining and twining,
And rattling and battling,
And shaking and quaking,
And pouring and roaring,
And waving and raving,
And tossing and crossing,
And flowing and going,
And running and stunning,
And foaming and roaming,
And dinning and spinning,
And dropping and hopping,
And working and jerking,
And guggling and struggling,
And heaving and cleaving,
And moaning and groaning;

And glittering and frittering,
And gathering and feathering,
And whitening and brightening,
And quivering and shivering,
And hurrying and skurrying,
And thundering and floundering;

Dividing and gliding and sliding,
And falling and brawling and sprawling,
And driving and riving and striving,
And sprinkling and twinkling and wrinkling,
And sounding and bounding and rounding,
And bubbling and troubling and doubling,
And grumbling and rumbling and tumbling,
And clattering and battering and shattering;

Retreating and beating and meeting and sheeting,
Delaying and straying and playing and spraying,
Advancing and prancing and glancing and dancing,
Recoiling, turmoiling and toiling and boiling,
And gleaming and streaming and steaming and beaming,
And rushing and flushing and brushing and gushing,
And flapping and rapping and clapping and slapping,
And curling and whirling and purling and twirling,
And thumping and plumping and bumping and jumping,
And dashing and flashing and splashing and clashing;
And so never ending, but always descending,
Sounds and motions for ever and ever are blending
All at once and all o'er, with a mighty uproar, –
And this way the water comes down at Lodore.

Robert Southey

Unit 5: How to have a debate

A debate is a discussion where two people, or two sides, offer opposing points of view on a topic. Each side is aiming to persuade the audience that theirs is the right view.

First choose a topic and decide who will support each side of the argument – who will speak for and who will speak against. Decide on a time limit for each speaker, for example two–three minutes.

The speakers

You won't necessarily get to put forward a point of view that agrees with your own; it is part of the skill of debating to be able to put forward a good argument in support of any viewpoint.

Plan and present your argument. List two–three good reasons in favour of your view. Explain each point using facts and examples. Try to include interesting/thought-provoking examples to get the audience's attention.

Present your argument using persuasive techniques:
- facts and figures
- persuasive and emotive language
- humour
- exaggeration
- repetition
- strong/commanding verbs.

The audience

The audience listens to each speech in turn. If there is time, the audience may ask questions of either side. The audience then votes for the argument that they think is more persuasive and convincing.

Unit 7: Book talk

Use these definitions to help you find out about the features of fiction and non-fiction books.

Feature	Explanation
afterword	Similar to a foreword but it comes after the main text. It often reflects on changes that have been made in a new edition or refers to recent events that are relevant to the book.
author's note	Some books contain a short note from the author to explain something about the book – like the period of history it is set in or something particular to look out for.
chapter	A section of a book, with or without a title. In non-fiction, each chapter covers a different topic. In fiction, chapters are episodes in the story – each episode has a beginning, a build-up to an issue or important event, and a climax or lead-in to the next chapter. Each new chapter signals a change in scene or direction in the main story.
contents	A list of the parts of a book (such as chapters, sections, parts, scenes) with the page numbers they start on. It comes at the beginning of the book.
epilogue	Only used in fiction books. It comes after the story either to tie up loose ends that may have been left in the story or to provide information from much later on that shows how events in the story turned out.
flashback	Stories normally work forwards as events take place one after another. A flashback interrupts the main story flow by going back to an earlier time. Flashbacks are events that happened in the past. They can be the narrator's own memories of an earlier time or seemingly separate events. The flashback always tells the reader something important connected to the main story.
foreword	Written by someone other than the author, such as a celebrity or someone who knows a lot about the subject or is well regarded. A foreword comes before the main text and usually praises the book and tells readers why they should read it. A foreword is always signed by the person who wrote it.
glossary	An alphabetical list of special terms or words used in a book that might not be familiar to everyone. Glossaries appear more in non-fiction books to explain any jargon used, but fiction books sometimes have a glossary, especially if local words are used that not everyone would understand.
index	A list of important words, concepts or other useful items that can be found in a book with page references to show where to find them. It comes at the end of the book.
plays	Rather than chapters, plays have acts and scenes. Short plays usually have only one act. The scenes are just what they sound like – a change of scene or action in the plot.
preface	Written by the author. A preface usually explains how the book came to be written or how the author got the idea for the book; it often includes thanks and acknowledgements to people who were helpful while it was being written.
prologue	Only used in fiction books. A prologue comes before the actual start of the story to introduce characters, explain past events or intrigue the reader by referring to a later event. Prologues should be short and use different features to interest the reader, such as: • a different perspective on events, using a different narrative voice to the main story • a flashback, giving the reader clues to help understand the events and characters • a flash-forward, revealing events from later in the story to build suspense for the reader, who imagines how the characters and plot get to that point.